WORLD CLASS
HOCKEY TRIVIA

DON WEEKES

GREYSTONE BOOKS

D&M PUBLISHERS INC.

Vancouver/Toronto/Berkeley

Greystone Books
An imprint of D&M Publishers Inc.
2323 Quebec Street, Suite 201
Vancouver BC Canada V5T 4S7
www.greystonebooks.com

Library and Archives Canada Cataloguing in Publication
Weekes, Don
World class hockey trivia / Don Weekes
ISBN 978-1-55365-484-1
1. Hockey—Miscellanea I. Title
GV847.W443 2009   796.962'66   C2009-904191-X

Editing by Derek Fairbridge
Cover and text design by Peter Cocking and Heather Pringle
Cover photograph by ©Reuters/CORBIS
Printed and bound in Canada by Friesens
Printed on paper that comes from sustainable forests
managed under the Forest Stewardship Council
Distributed in the U.S. by Publishers Group West

We gratefully acknowledge the financial support of the Canada Council
for the Arts, the British Columbia Arts Council, the Province of British Columbia
through the Book Publishing Tax Credit and the Government of Canada
through the Book Publishing Industry Development Program (BPIDP)
for our publishing activities.

Mixed Sources
Cert no. SW-COC-001271
© 1996 FSC
FSC

CONTENTS

INTRODUCTION

IT BEGAN ON AN undersized patch of natural ice called Le Palais de Glace at the 1920 Olympics in Antwerp, Belgium. The overflow crowd of the curious, either lucky enough to get tickets or steal their way into the small figure skating rink, became unwitting witnesses to the birth of international hockey. That this tournament of seven-man hockey was staged at the Summer Games (the Winter Olympics didn't exist yet) as a demonstration sport, made it all the more remarkable. European clubs had been sparring on and off for a decade, but this was the first time Canada and USA brought their North American puck game to continental ice. The result was a Canadian gold medal for the Winnipeg Falcons, a team of outsiders in their own country who made hockey history as the first true world champions.

The Falcons' ascent to Olympic glory is a classic story of triumph over adversity—the kind of story that makes the world game so fascinating, no matter what team you cheer for and anthem you sing in the international arena. These second-generation Canadians, sons of Icelandic immigrants, overcame discrimination at home to become their nation's representatives abroad, and, ultimately, they returned as conquering heroes. Yes, it occurred long ago, but over the fullness of time their storyline is as dramatic as any in our endlessly compelling history of the game.

In fact, the Falcons' dream was no different than most kids' dreams of playing in the big leagues; nor dissimilar to the ambitions of all athletes. The narrative repeats itself at the 1954 World Championships, when the Soviet Union shocked Canada and the world, and began the most dominating era in international hockey. Later, it happened to a young American squad of amateur collegians, who felled the powerful Soviets and sent an entire nation into a frenzy in 1980. And then it was tiny Slovakia's turn in the spotlight after that fledgling country, over a few short years, played its way from the C Pool to its first world title in 2002.

In *World Class Hockey Trivia*, we take a skate through hockey history to discover the remarkable exploits of Connie Broden, Vsevolod Bobrov and the Triple Gold Club. Along the way we bring to life the ideals of the amateur sport of Father David Bauer; all-world goalie Dominik Hasek's clinic on puck-stopping at the first Olympics to feature full NHL participation; the headline-grabbing defections of Alexander Mogilny and the Stastny brothers from behind the Iron Curtain to NHL freedom; and Paul Henderson's heroics at the legendary 1972 Summit Series, the first of several best-on-best competitions that still resonate with fans because of what hockey writer Joe Pelletier calls, "the special mystique of the old tournaments."

It is for all these reasons that we thought it was time to take our NHL-inspired *Hockey Trivia* series to the international level. Not only for the spectacle on ice and the richness of its rivalries, but because of how international play transformed the sport, merging European finesse with the brutal majesty of North American play into the real beauty of the world game we enjoy today.

DON WEEKES
June 2009

I

HOCKEY NIGHT ON PLANET EARTH

WHO IS CAPTAIN CANADA? What qualifications are required for membership in the Triple Gold Club? When did Europeans first play hockey, North American–style? In our opening chapter of general questions, we challenge your trivia mojo on everything from the most lopsided score on record to the finest game ever played. Along the way, we check out some of the world game's greatest superheroes, its most villainous act and the nastiest dictator ever to rule behind the bench. Then, we size up your shot on a hat trick of historic firsts that changed the sport's rulebook; and several defining moments that tore down the wall separating the NHL universe from the "other" hockey played on the international stage. Comrades, sharpen your blades and sickles, and say hello to Hockey Night on Planet Earth.

Answers are on page 8

1.1   Which country achieved an international first with a double gold, winning the Olympics and World Championships in the same year?
    A.   The Soviet Union in 1972
    B.   Czechoslovakia in 1976
    C.   Canada in 2002
    D.   Sweden in 2006

1.2   What was Bobby Orr's only major outing in world competition?
    A.   The 1968 Winter Olympics
    B.   The 1972 Summit Series
    C.   The 1976 Canada Cup
    D.   Bobby Orr never played international hockey

1.3   What sport in Europe declined in popularity after North American hockey was introduced there during the 1920s?
    A.   Bandy
    B.   Lacrosse
    C.   Hurley
    D.   Shinty

.... 3 ....

1.4 What rule was implemented by the NHL immediately after it was first
tried at the 2002 Olympics?

A. No-touch icing
B. The two-referee system
C. The elimination of the centre red line for two-line passes
D. The hurry-up faceoff

1.5 Who was the first player to be nicknamed Captain Canada?

A. Steve Yzerman
B. Shane Doan
C. Joe Sakic
D. Ryan Smyth

1.6 In what year did Canada and the Soviet Union play against each other
for the first time?

A. 1934
B. 1944
C. 1954
D. 1964

1.7 Jaroslav Drobny, a star forward with the 1947 World Championship
Czechoslovak team, was a two-sport athlete who won major titles in
his "other" game, including which one?

A. Swimming's 100-metre freestyle at the Olympics
B. Tennis' Wimbledon tournament
C. Auto racing's Le Mans
D. Golf's U.S. Open

1.8 Prior to the establishment of a national team program in the early
1960s, the winning team of which trophy usually represented Canada
internationally?

A. The Memorial Cup
B. The Stanley Cup
C. The Canada Cup
D. The Allan Cup

1.9 Who was Father David Bauer?

A. He established Canada's national team program
B. He led the development of hockey across Europe

C. He was the first chair of the board for Hockey Canada

D. He coached the first Canadian hockey team to wear the famous red maple leaf

1.10 How many games did Canadian-born Hayley Wickenheiser play before scoring her first goal with the Kirkkonummi Salamat of Finland's Mestis league in 2002–03?

A. One game

B. Three games

C. Six games

D. Wickenheiser never scored a goal in 2002–03

1.11 What historic rule change was implemented by the International Ice Hockey Federation (IIHF) in 1969?

A. Curved sticks were permitted

B. Bodychecking was allowed in all three zones

C. Helmets were mandatory

D. Goaltenders could not play the puck outside the crease

1.12 Who is Seth Martin?

A. The first Canadian captain with an Olympic gold medal

B. The American who coached Czechoslovakia in 1948

C. The American forward with two Olympic scoring titles

D. The Canadian goalie who influenced a generation of European netminders

1.13 What is the "Punch-up in Piestany"?

A. A fracas at the 1972 Summit Series

B. A nickname for a Czechoslovak checking line

C. A brawl at the 1987 World Junior Championships

D. A fighting tactic used by the Soviets at the Canada Cup

1.14 Which country iced the first members of the Triple Gold Club by winning hockey's three most prestigious championships: the Olympics, the Stanley Cup and the World Championships?

A. Finland

B. Sweden

C. Canada

D. Russia

1.15 Old-timer Connie Broden can claim which hockey first?

    A. The first winner of a Stanley Cup and a World Championship

    B. The first winner of a Stanley Cup and an Olympic gold medal

    C. The first winner of a Stanley Cup and a World Championship in the same year

    D. The first winner of a Stanley Cup and an Olympic gold medal in the same year

1.16 Prior to 2010, how many players have won a Stanley Cup and an Olympic gold medal in the same year?

    A. Three players

    B. Five players

    C. Seven players

    D. 11 players

1.17 Which country's top-ranked team is named Tre Kronor?

    A. Slovakia

    B. Finland

    C. Norway

    D. Sweden

1.18 In what series did Canadian-born Brett Hull first play for the USA?

    A. The 1986 World Championships

    B. The 1992 Canada Cup

    C. The 1996 World Cup of Hockey

    D. The 1998 Olympics

1.19 Who is recognized as the first player to complain publicly about coach Viktor Tikhonov's iron fist rule over the Soviet squads during the 1980s?

    A. Sergei Makarov

    B. Alexei Kasatonov

    C. Igor Larionov

    D. Viacheslav Fetisov

1.20 Which country's national team iced the "Green Unit"?

    A. The Soviet Union

    B. USA

    C. Canada

    D. Sweden

1.21 In what many consider the finest hockey game ever played, the
Montreal Canadiens and the Soviet Red Army battled to a 3–3 tie
in their epic New Year's Eve game of 1975. What was the final shot
count between the two clubs?
   A. 38–13 in favour of the Montreal Canadiens
   B. 31–21 in favour of the Montreal Canadiens
   C. 31–21 in favour of the Soviet Red Army
   D. 38–13 in favour of the Soviet Red Army

1.22 What is the most lopsided score ever recorded in top-group
competition of men's hockey?
   A. 17–0
   B. 27–0
   C. 37–0
   D. 47–0

1.23 Which major rule change did the IIHF implement in May 1998?
   A. Crease rules were revised to protect the goalie
   B. High-sticking was redefined
   C. The red line was dropped to allow the two-line pass
   D. Video replays were employed on questionable goals

1.24 To celebrate their 100th anniversary, the IIHF produced the *IIHF Top
100 Hockey Stories of All Time.* What story ranked first?
   A. Sweden's unique double-gold victories in 2006
   B. USA's "Miracle on Ice" triumph during the 1980 Olympics
   C. Paul Henderson's series winner against the Soviet Union
      during the 1972 Summit Series
   D. Great Britain's surprise gold medal at the 1936 Olympics

1.25 In December 2006, a high-profile charity game featuring Soviet and
NHL greats was played in Moscow's Red Square. What was the age of
the youngest player who participated in that old-timers match?
   A. 10 years old
   B. 25 years old
   C. 35 years old
   D. 55 years old

Hockey Night on Planet Earth

1.1 D. Sweden in 2006

Considering Canada and the Soviet Union's long dominance in international hockey, Sweden's double gold at the Turin Olympics and Riga World Championships in 2006 is truly historic. No team in the six previous occasions when the Worlds and Winter Games were held in the same year managed to lock up both titles. Sweden completed the double victory three months after claiming Olympic gold in a heart-stopping 3–2 win against Nordic-rival Finland in February 2006. But the Swedes entered the Worlds minus the gut of their Olympic team, including goalie hero Henrik Lundqvist and three players that defined Sweden as a hockey superpower and produced the gold-medal-winning goal: Nicklas Lidstrom, Peter Forsberg and Mats Sundin. Now their nation's hockey program itself would be tested as only eight Olympians returned to play in the World Championships. In the early rounds the Swedes were defeated just once, in a 5–2 loss to Slovakia. Then, they walloped USA 6–0 and held on in a 5–4 win against Canada before their 4–0 victory for the gold medal against the Czech Republic. The eight gold medalists who shared in this double feat are: Henrik Zetterberg, Jorgen Jonsson, Kenny Jonsson, Niklas Kronwall, Mika Hannula, Mikael Samuelsson, Ronnie Sundin and backup goalie Stefan Liv.

1.2 C. The 1976 Canada Cup

The only time world hockey experienced the gamesmanship of Bobby Orr was at the inaugural Canada Cup in 1976. What North American fans had been treated to in his grace, speed and deftness of play at the NHL level could now be appreciated by fans around the world as Orr played against the best players on the planet. Orr missed 1972's Summit Series between Canada and the Soviet Union, but he would not forego the international challenge of 1976. He scored a tournament-high nine points in seven games and won MVP honours; all the while playing on knees so ravaged from surgery that his joints were little more than bone rubbing on bone. Regrettably, it was his last great moment of glory. Over the next three seasons, No. 4 played just 26 NHL games for the Chicago Blackhawks. He retired for good in 1979 after an all-too-brief 12-year career that included this lone heroic performance on the world scene.

1.3 A. Bandy

North American–style hockey made its grand entrance to European audiences at the 1920 Summer Olympics in Antwerp, Belgium. Olympic organizers said that if Canada participated, they would put hockey in the program. Six other countries iced teams, including the USA, Czechoslovakia and Sweden. Until then, Europeans had been playing a form of field hockey on ice known as bandy, using short curved sticks and a ball. In fact, every member of the Swedish team at those Olympics was a bandy player using a puck for the first time; and they wore speed skates and did not have the same skill at starting and stopping as the Canadian players. Further, they had little upper body protection, crude gloves, no shin pads and dressed like soccer players, except for the goalie who wore "a cross between a blacksmith's apron and an aviator's coat," according to William Hewitt, who officiated the event. But what the Europeans lacked in skating ability and on-ice strategy, they made up for in physical play and enthusiasm. For their part, the North Americans put on a show of hockey skills that so thrilled audiences, it launched the sport in Europe and gave rise to the international game. Moreover, Olympic authorities were so encouraged by the competition, they established a separate Olympics for winter sports with a more organized event in 1924.

1.4 D. The hurry-up faceoff

The pace and style of play at the 2002 Olympics so impressed NHL general managers that within weeks of the tournament, the league adopted the hurry-up faceoff for the 2002—03 season. The IIHF rule eliminated the strategy of stalling for time after a whistle by granting each team just five seconds to make a line change, first by the visitors, followed by the home side; and another five seconds for players to be in position and on-side before the puck was dropped. The NHL adapted the rule to allow visitors five seconds and the home team eight seconds, with the puck drop happening five seconds after that. As a result, time spent during play stoppages was kept to a minimum and matches could be played in about two hours. Unfortunately, the NHL stopped short of embracing two other rules at the Winter Games: no-touch icing and the two-line offside. It was the elimination of the centre red line for two-line passes that truly sped up the action at the 2002 Olympics and had critics calling the Games "the best hockey tournament ever held." The NHL finally adopted this rule in 2005–06; but have not, at this writing, implemented no-touch icing.

1.5   D. Ryan Smyth

While Shane Doan was making a strong case to be dubbed Captain Canada in his third stint wearing the "C" for Canada at the 2009 World Championships, it was Ryan Smyth who first earned the superhero title when he represented his country in seven Worlds, two Olympics and one World Cup of Hockey. Playing for the once-lackluster Edmonton Oilers, a team that failed to qualify for the postseason or lost the preliminary playoff round each year from 1999 to 2005, gave Smyth the opportunities to prove himself on international ice. Smyth captained Canada for five straight years between 2001 and 2005 at the Worlds, bringing home two gold medals and a silver, and wore Olympic gold on his chest in 2002, followed by another gold at the World Cup of Hockey in 2004. His first taste of international victory came with a gold medal for Canada at the 1995 World Juniors, an experience that left an indelible impression on the 19-year-old. "I've played for my country before," Smyth told the *Toronto Sun*, "and there is nothing better than standing out there hearing that national anthem being played. Nothing." Smyth appeared in every international senior game between 1999 and 2006, a record 78 matches, scoring 18 goals and 37 points in Canada's battle for world supremacy.

1.6   C. 1954

The first meeting between Canada and the Soviet Union came in the final game of the 1954 World Championships. Canada was represented by the Toronto Lyndhursts, just a Senior B team, but still good enough to rack up an undefeated streak of six victories against their world opponents. All that stood in their way of another gold medal was a tie against a Soviet squad of unknowns, with names such as Bobrov, Guryshev and Kuzin. Each player was a product of

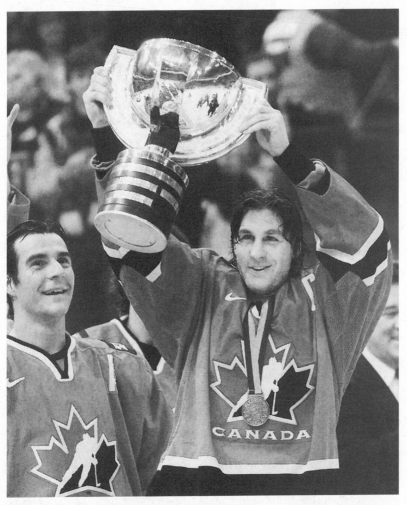

Team Canada captain Ryan Smyth holds up the 2004 World Championship trophy in Prague. Teammate Steve Staios looks on, as Canada captured its second straight gold-medal title.

a hockey program that was started from scratch only eight years earlier by Anatoli Tarasov. With little more than a few technical handbooks on the game, Tarasov converted his nation's best bandy players to hockey, inventing a weave-and-pass style of play based on speed, skating and stick work. Their success didn't come overnight, but backed by the country's political authorities, hockey went from being branded "a capitalist sport" in the 1920s and 1930s to their national game after 1946, when hockey officially began in the Soviet Union. The results in 1954 were a shocker as Tarasov's troops routed Canada 7–2 in their first World Championships to claim the gold medal. Toronto's Conn Smythe was so infuriated by the loss that he wanted to take his Maple Leafs to Europe to recapture the title. Canada now had a true international rival. The balance of power in the hockey world had changed forever.

1.7   B. Tennis' Wimbledon tournament

Given the high calibre of competition in sports today, it's unlikely any current athlete could match the wild success of Jaroslav Drobny, who was once a world champion in both hockey and tennis. By comparison, Drobny's feat today would be like Mike Modano collecting his 2002 Olympic silver medal and then storming through the field of tennis' French Open to challenge Albert Costa at centre court in the singles final. But that's exactly what Drobny accomplished in 1948. Only a few weeks after leading his Czechoslovak squad to the silver medal at the combined Olympics and World Championships tournament, he reached his second Grand Slam final at the French championships, losing to Frank Parker in four sets on the clay of Stade Roland Garros. But his simultaneous successes in two disciplines soon meant one sport would suffer. By 1949, tennis had become his full-time passion and Drobny was playing fewer national team games. He also passed on an opportunity to be the first European-trained NHLer when the Boston Bruins came calling in 1949, because "By going to the NHL, I would have lost the chance to play in international tennis tournaments," as Drobny once said. Instead, he vaulted to the top 10 in world tennis, reaching the Wimbledon finals twice before capturing the event in 1954, the first left-hander to do so and for a long time afterwards the only native Czech to claim the famous British tennis title.

1.8   D. The Allan Cup

Before Canada started sending professional players to world tournaments, it was usually represented internationally by their best amateur team. Typically this meant the Allan Cup champions, amateur hockey's top club at the national senior level. (The trophy was strictly for amateur teams and in 1909 replaced the Stanley Cup, which had become a professional competition.)

Teams such as the Toronto Granites (1923), Penticton Vees (1954) and Kitchener-Waterloo Dutchmen (1955) routinely won cups and medals abroad after capturing the Allan Cup hockey championship at home. While the seniors performed a notch below NHL-calibre players, their skill level was considerable, given that there were only six teams in the NHL prior to 1967 and few other options besides pro leagues, including the American Hockey League. Later, the honour of representing Canada alternated between Allan Cup finalists from the east and west; and, then, by a combination of top players from across the country.

1.9 A. He established Canada's national team program

Father David Bauer was a hockey coach and builder who just happened to choose the priesthood over a professional sports career. Born into a hockey-playing family, Bauer (his brother Bobby was on the Boston Bruins' famous "Kraut Line") attended St. Michael's College in Toronto and won a Memorial Cup while on loan to the Oshawa Generals in 1944. In 1953, after his ordination as a priest, he returned to St. Mike's as a teacher and a coach of the school's junior squad, which went on to win a Memorial Cup in 1961 under his guidance. After a transfer to St. Mark's College at the University of British Columbia (UBC) in 1962, he petitioned the Canadian Amateur Hockey Association (CAHA) to establish a national team program of top amateurs that would compete globally, instead of a system using club representation, which often was Canada's best senior team—the winners of the Allan Cup. Bauer believed in the ideals of amateur sport and that young Canadians could play at elite levels while receiving a formal education. The CAHA approved Father Bauer's proposal and Canada's national team was created, made up of UBC students such as Brian Conacher, Roger Bourbonnais and Marshall Johnston. Against ever-stronger competition from Europe, Bauer's Canadian teams won bronze medals at the 1966 and 1967 World Championships and an Olympic bronze at Grenoble, France in 1968. But his national program was soon disbanded as a result of Canada's opposition to amateur-only teams at international events. In 1986, an Olympic rink in Calgary was dedicated to him and three years later he was elected in the builder category to the Hockey Hall of Fame.

1.10 C. Six games

Hayley Wickenheiser, former star of Canada's national team and sometimes known as the "female Wayne Gretzky," scored her first goal in her sixth game with Kirkkonummi, a third-division semi-pro club from Finland. Her historic marker—and an assist—came in a 5–4 loss on February 1, 2003. "I was the only girl out there and I had to give my best everyday," said Wickenheiser. "Anything less wasn't successful. I had something to prove." Although Wickenheiser became the first woman to play full-time professional hockey at a position other than goalie and the first to score a goal in a men's pro hockey league, it was not a great stretch for her, considering Hayley played on boys' teams until she was 12 years old. She finished 2002–03 with 12 points, including two goals, in 23 games.

1.11 B. Bodychecking was allowed in all three zones

As bizarre as it may seem today, for nearly a half century of international hockey, hitting was forbidden on certain parts of the ice. Previous to 1969, when the rule was amended to align the IIHF with NHL play, bodychecking was allowed only in the defensive zone and only by a defenseman on his attacker. Forwards were not allowed to hit a defenseman in his zone and there was no hitting by anyone in the neutral zone. Why was the rule in place? Apparently, it was a matter of safety for defensemen picking up loose pucks in their own zone, but with rules that were designed to affect all three zones of play, it probably came from European fears of turning the game into "a sport of goons," as IIHF president Bunny Ahearne often said. To be fair, Ahearne wasn't completely wrong, because European players would have to adjust their style and play a more aggressive game to meet the demands of physical contact in any zone. That didn't mean goon hockey, just a more fairly played contest with equal rules all over the ice. Clearly, Ahearne's old-world view of amateur hockey didn't include one of the game's most exciting qualities, the art of intimidation by hitting, which often forced costly mistakes and turnovers to create scoring opportunities. For North Americans, the rule change meant one less adjustment at the world level. They didn't have to think where they could give a hit or take one. It was now everywhere on the ice.

1.12   **D. The Canadian goalie who influenced a generation of European netminders**

When the Soviets began playing hockey they learned by watching and studying individuals such as Lloyd Percival, the coach and author of *The Hockey Handbook*, which is still considered by some as the definitive technical book on the game. Among rising netminders during the 1960s, including the Soviet's Vladislav Tretiak and Czech legend Jiri Holecek, one individual to emulate was Canada's Seth Martin. Less known by fans today, he was once the most popular Canadian player in Europe. And the most studied and copied by European goalies who saw Martin as a role model of style and reliability. He backstopped Canada in multiple events during the 1960s, but his greatest impact on the sport may have been influencing Tretiak, Holecek and others, who, themselves, would influence another generation, including goaltenders such as Vladimir Dzurilla, Pelle Lindbergh and Dominik Hasek.

1.13   **C. A brawl at the 1987 World Junior Championships**

On the night of January 4, 1987, the hockey world became party to an act so unfamiliarly violent in its breadth that it earned a reputation as the gravest melee in the international game. The all-out clash minted a new generation of hockey thugs on fan consciousness, deprived a nation of a championship title and, if you accept Gare Joyce's position in the definitive work *When the Lights Went Out*, ended hockey's Cold War and changed the sport forever. How it all started at the arena in Piestany, Czechoslovakia, even Joyce can't conclusively say, but Evgeny Davydov was first player from either team to leave his bench and join a second-period melee sparked by a slash from Soviet forward Pavel Kostichkin on Canadian Theo Fleury. Going into the game, the Soviets had nothing to lose and were out of medal contention after a rare bad tournament with just two wins, three losses and a tie. Meanwhile, the gold medal was at stake for Canada's juniors but they needed to score at least five goals in the game; any fewer assured them of only a silver to Finland's gold. Canada was applying the pressure, trying to increase the 4–2 lead in the second period when everything fell apart. Canadian and Soviet players, fed up with stick work and running at each other, dropped their gloves and engaged in a 20-minute brawl that cleared both benches. With the fight out of control, the officials left the ice and ordered the arena lights dimmed. Order was eventually restored but the game was lost. Afterwards, Soviet officials blamed a Canadian trainer for fuelling the hostilities, while Canada accused the Soviets of starting the brawl by leaving their bench first with the intention of getting Canada disqualified. When sentencing was meted out, both teams were disqualified, players were suspended for 18 months (but that was later rescinded) and their records erased. Canada lost the gold, which went under odd circumstances to Finland.

1.14   **B. Sweden**
The first inductees into the Triple Gold Club were Tomas Jonsson, Mats Naslund and Hakan Loob. They became founding members on February 27, 1994 in Lillehammer, Norway, when Sweden won its first Olympic gold medal. All three Swedes also captured gold at the 1991 World Championships (Loob earned another in 1987) and the Stanley Cup, as Jonsson won with the New York Islanders in 1982 and 1983, Naslund with Montreal in 1986 and Loob with Calgary in 1989. Since its debut in 1994, the club membership has swelled to an all-star lineup that includes Igor Larionov, Joe Sakic and Jaromir Jagr. Who took the shortest time to win all three titles? In a span of two years, Sweden's Niklas Kronwall, Henrik Zetterberg and Mikael Samuelsson claimed double golds at the Worlds and Olympics in 2006, followed by a Stanley Cup with Detroit in 2008. In contrast, it took Viacheslav Fetisov 19 years from his first victory to become a member.

1.15   **C. The first winner of a Stanley Cup and World Championship in the same year**
Little-known Connie Broden never belonged to the prestigious Triple Gold Club, but he accomplished something no one else achieved in that fraternity when he became the first and only player crowned world champion and Stanley Cup champion in the same season. It came at a time when amateurs and pros could move, given the skills and circumstances, between playing levels. And that was Broden's fortune when he decided to retire rather than play with the Montreal Canadiens' farm team in the

American Hockey League in 1957–58. The Whitby Dunlops' senior team of the Ontario Hockey League approached Canadiens management for his services and they obliged. When the Dunlops went to the World Championships in Oslo, Norway, Broden was there to play a key role in their gold-medal victory with a tournament-high 19 points. One month later, Broden was in the Canadiens lineup as a spare during their six-game march against Boston to the Stanley Cup. He saw action in only one match, but that qualified him as Cup winner. No one has duplicated his accomplishment since, but a few players have won Olympic gold and Stanley Cup silver in the same year.

1.16   A. Three players

It's unlikely anyone will ever join Connie Broden as a double champion with gold at the World Championships and Olympics in a single season, but every Olympic year athletes get another chance to enter the ranks of Ken Morrow, Steve Yzerman and Brendan Shanahan as Olympic gold medalists and Stanley Cup winners. Morrow established this class of double winner in 1980 as a defenseman on USA at the Lake Placid Olympics and, later that spring, with the New York Islanders' championship squad. Yzerman and Shanahan increased the membership to three by both playing with Canada and the Detroit Red Wings in 2002. On the 2006 Stanley Cup champion Carolina Hurricanes, only Niclas Wallin was a Swedish national but he was left off Sweden's Olympic gold-medal roster that year.

1.17   D. Sweden

Olympic teams such as Canada and USA have typically taken their national symbols and incorporated them into the designs of their jerseys. A prime example is Canada's famous maple leaf, which has been a Canuck standard since the first Olympics in 1920. Sweden's logo dates to the 1938 World Championships, when its national team's sweater first featured the Tre Kronor, which means "three crowns" and refers to the trio of blue crowns (positioned two above and one below) placed on a yellow background. It is the national emblem of Sweden.

1.18 A. The 1986 World Championships

Born in Belleville, Ontario, and raised in Chicago and Winnipeg, Brett Hull played for USA on several occasions, starting with the 1986 World Championships. With dual citizenship, Hull could play for either Canada or America but chose USA throughout his international career after Canadian coach Dave King said he couldn't skate well enough to represent Canada in 1986. Hull, who was playing at the University of Minnesota Duluth at the time, accepted the offer to play from USA coach Dave Peterson and never looked anywhere else when his adopted country sought him out for future tournaments. Typically, Hull was as outspoken about the world game as about NHL hockey. He based his allegiance to a team, not a flag, as he said more than once. "I hate the whole anthem aspect of the tournament," said Hull about the 1991 Canada Cup. "We're not going to war; we're playing hockey. Right wing is my hockey position, not a statement of my political beliefs. I went looking for good hockey, not global supremacy for my country." Hull competed at the 1991 Canada Cup, won silver at the 2002 Olympics and the World Cup of Hockey in 1996.

1.19 C. Igor Larionov

It was an act of defiance that may have mirrored the changing state of affairs in Russian society at the time, but for the regimented hockey world of Viktor Tikhonov, Igor Larionov's open letter of protest (published in the widely circulated magazine, *Ogonyok*), it meant revolution. How controlling was Tikhonov of his Red Army recruits? NHL coaches such as Mike Keenan and Scotty Bowman, even during their most fiendish days behind the bench, never wielded such absolute power. While Bowman and Keenan became masters of manipulation to gain success on the ice, Tikhonov's diabolical machinations touched all aspects of his players' lives. His old-fashioned, hard-line methods had team members in endless practices and conditioning drills up to 11 months of the year, all while confined to training-camp barracks with little time off, even for married players. Finally, it was Larionov, one third of the famed "KLM Line," who wrote a lengthy letter about Tikhonov's authoritarian rule "to open society's eyes to what was really being done in this system." For his actions, Larionov paid an immediate price. He was cut from the team, but not before captain

Team USA's Brett Hull controls the puck against Russia during the 19th Winter Olympic Games in Salt Lake City. Hull's eight points in six games led the Americans to the silver medal.

Viacheslav Fetisov joined him in protest. The once-invincible "Big Red Machine" was broken and in chaos. Only a promise by the Soviet authorities to allow player movement to the NHL salvaged the 1989 World Championships in Stockholm. But it was the last tournament to feature all the best Soviet players. Under glasnost, the new Soviet political policy of openness, Tikhonov's players left in droves, lured by the prospects of playing in the West.

1.20 A. The Soviet Union

When legendary coach Scotty Bowman iced the NHL's first five-man unit of Russians on the Detroit Red Wings in the late 1990s, he was paying the ultimate compliment of imitation to the old Soviet hockey system. Bowman figured if the combination of three forwards and two defensemen could work so effectively as one unit for the Red Army team, CSKA Moscow, during the 1980s, it should reap rewards for his Red Wings squad. He was right, of course, as Detroit set an NHL record with 62 wins in 1995–96 and then captured back-to-back Stanley Cups, using in North America a formula that had been so successful for the Soviets when the famed "Green Unit" of Viacheslav Fetisov, Alexei Kasatonov, Sergei Makarov, Igor Larionov and Vladimir Krutov led the national team to four World Championships in 1982, 1983, 1986 and 1989 and two Olympic gold medals in 1984 and 1988. Known as the "Green Unit" because they wore green jerseys in practice, the five-man group was a dominant force in European hockey until they were split up in 1989 when Soviet emigration restrictions eased under glasnost and each received permission to play in the NHL. Their new careers had mixed results. Krutov was a bust after just one season in Vancouver and returned to the European leagues; both Makarov, who won the Calder as top NHL rookie in 1990, and Kasatonov were out of the NHL by 1997; while Fetisov and Larionov played on Bowman's feared "Red Army Line" (with Sergei Fedorov, Vyacheslav Kozlov and Vladimir Konstantinov) and became the centrepiece of Detroit's two Cups in 1997 and 1998. Larionov won a third Cup with the Red Wings in 2002 and retired in 2004.

1.21 **A. 38–13 in favour of the Montreal Canadiens**

It was merely an exhibition game but for any one of the 18,975 fans at the Montreal Forum that night or the millions of television viewers watching around the world, it is still remembered as the greatest hockey game ever played. The Montreal Canadiens and the Soviet Red Army were arguably the world's two finest hockey clubs of their era; and had many of the game's best players playing at their peak. The Canadiens possessed a future-hall-of-fame lineup in Guy Lafleur, Bob Gainey, Serge Savard and Ken Dryden, all on the verge of beginning their march to four consecutive Stanley Cups later that season. CSKA Moscow's powerhouse squad of Olympic fame featured a superbly tuned machine of talent in Vladislav Tretiak, Valeri Kharlamov and Boris Mikhailov.

Still, on this New Year's Eve night in 1975, the Canadiens dominated the Soviets everywhere but on the scoreboard and between the pipes. Dryden gave up three goals on the 13 shots that got through the "Big Three" on defense of Savard, Larry Robinson and Guy Lapointe. At the other end, the incomparable Tretiak was brilliant and his play that night "put him into the Hockey Hall of Fame," opined Dick Irvin, a member of the Hall's selection committee. The Soviet netminder was fired upon 38 times and despite each team's distinct style of play—the finesse passing game of the Soviets versus the shoot-at-will Canadian brand—the shots Tretiak stopped were all quality shots. According to referee Wally Harris, who officiated the 3–3 standoff, Tretiak never once made the first move on any shooter. "I can't remember a goaltender who could stare down the guys the way he did that night," said Harris in Irvin's *The Habs*. In one flurry, with the Soviets two men short, Tretiak stopped three rapid-fire, point-blank shots before giving up a Montreal goal to Yvan Cournoyer, who played a pivotal role a few years earlier in 1972's famed Summit Series. For Cournoyer, the 1975 New Year's match was 1972 all over again. Only this time everyone knew what to expect, including all the emotion and pressure that came with it. Was it the greatest game ever? With Montreal decisively outplaying the Soviets by a 38–13 shot count, some preferred to call it the greatest lopsided game ever.

1.22 D. 47–0

International hockey has had its share of mismatched opponents and blowouts, but nothing compares to the lopsided score of 47–0 racked up by Canada against Denmark in their opening game at the 1949 World Championships. Forty-seven to zero. This isn't a hockey score. It's annihilation by puck. But the real crime was in letting newcomers such as the Danes onto the same ice surface with Canada's national team. So what did the game look like? The Danish squad rarely advanced past the centre red line as Canada applied a game-long stranglehold on their goalmouth, amassing 13 goals in the first period, 16 in the second and 18 in the third. All 11 Canadian skaters potted at least a hat trick, with Jim Russell leading the way with eight goals. According to local press reports, "Spectators laughed heartily at the Danish efforts to make a game of it. The chief thrill for the crowd was betting on whether Canada would top 50 goals or not." How badly did the Danes take the humiliation? Let's just say that Denmark didn't return to elite international competition for more than a half-century, until the 2003 Worlds. They finished in 11th place in the 16-team tournament that year, but, in their first game back, stunned USA with a 5–2 win in the preliminary round and, later, got some payback in a startling 2–2 tie against Canada, their 1949 vanquishers. Today, Denmark has only a small hockey following and about 4,000 players of all ages.

1.23 C. The red line was dropped to allow the two-line pass

When the IIHF approved the removal of the red line to permit two-line passes, it took the advantage away from defense-dominated teams and opened up the ice for more creative offense. Consequently, it made the game less boring for fans who had seen their sport regress to defensive tactics borrowed from European soccer formations that made it hard to penetrate the offensive zone. On ice, that system became the neutral-zone trap, whereby defenders clogged mid-ice to kill attack momentum by opponents. It proved to be a goal killer, too. Still, dropping the red line didn't happen quickly. The IIHF Congress began discussions during the 1980s and only made it a reality when IIHF president René Fasel persuaded voting delegates to test such a rule at major tournaments in 1997–98. The following year fans got their first taste of how exciting hockey could be when the new rule finally eliminated the centre line for two-line passes. It would be another seven years before it was implemented in the NHL.

1.24 C. USA's "Miracle on Ice" triumph during the 1980 Olympics

The IIHF evaluated their top 100 stories based on their influence and impact on world hockey. The story could be about a tournament or game, player or moment, including a goal or a great save, but always at the highest level of play, notably the Olympics or the World Championships. In this regard, after 100 years of hockey, the IIHF selected America's historic 4–3 win versus the Soviet Union in 1980 as their number one story, followed by Paul Henderson's heroics in Game 8 of the 1972 Summit Series and, in third spot, the Soviets' shocking 7–3 win against Canada in the

Summit Series opener. In defense of its top selection, the IIHF authors said USA's victory literally defined Olympic success, that a squad of college players could defeat an international hockey dynasty was in a sporting sense "a miracle"; and that the historic win changed United States hockey history forever, inspiring the next generation of American kids to dream of being hockey champions. Not surprisingly, at the World Cup of Hockey in 1996, many players on the Cup-winning American squad cited 1980 as their inspiration for playing the game.

1.25   A. 10 years old

To celebrate three Russian milestones (the 60th anniversary of the birth of Russian hockey, the 50th anniversary of the former Soviet Union's first Olympic gold medal in hockey and the 25th anniversary of the famous KLM Line in the 1980s), a charity game between former Soviet greats and old NHLers was played for the first time ever in Moscow's Red Square. An outdoor rink with seating for 2,000 fans was built for the event, just a slapshot from Lenin's Tomb, the onion-domed Saint Basil's Cathedral and Spassky Tower. Scotty Bowman coached Team World, made up of NHL stars such as Jari Kurri, Paul Coffey and Peter Stastny. The Russians included the best of old Soviet hockey: Igor Larionov, Sergei Makarov and Viacheslav Fetisov. Midway through the game of three 15-minute periods, Maxim Tretiak, the 10-year-old grandson of legendary netminder Vladislav Tretiak, stepped between the pipes and played six shutout minutes against Team World. The historic event ended in a 10-10 draw.

The Triple Gold Club

THE THREE MOST IMPORTANT championships available in hockey are the Olympic Games, World Championships and Stanley Cup. In our game, fill in the blanks with the years each member of the Triple Gold Club *first* achieved each of the game's highest honours.

Solutions are on page 138

OLYMPICS:
1984   1988   1994   1998   2002   2006

WORLD CHAMPIONSHIPS:
1982   1987   1989   1991   1992   1994   1997   2005   2006

STANLEY CUPS:
1989   1991   1996   1997   2000   2007   2008

	OLYMPICS	WORLD CHAMPIONSHIPS	STANLEY CUPS
Nicklas Lidstrom			
Brendan Shanahan			
Jaromir Jagr			
Alexander Mogilny			
Joe Sakic			
Henrik Zetterberg			
Hakan Loob			
Chris Pronger			
Peter Forsberg			
Igor Larionov			

2

SUMMIT SHOWDOWN

THE 1972 SUMMIT SERIES was never just about the hockey. The eight-game exhibition tournament was supposed to determine hockey supremacy between Canada and the Soviets, but it turned into something much more than what either side expected. Communism and capitalism were competing on the same ice, in the same arenas and at the same time as hockey history was being shaped. It was our Dominion versus the Evil Empire or as Paul Henderson said: "It was Canada playing, not Team Canada. It was us against them and every Canadian somehow seemed to have a sense of ownership of that team." Nothing, before or since, has transcended the boundaries of sport like that Canada-Soviet showdown in September 1972. More than just the game changed. Ask anyone who was around at the time.

Answers are on page 31

2.1   How many shots were fired on net before the first goal was scored at the 1972 Summit Series?

  A.   One shot on net
  B.   Two shots on net
  C.   Four shots on net
  D.   Six shots on net

2.2   Which NHL team was most represented among the 35 players originally selected to Team Canada?

  A.   The Boston Bruins
  B.   The Montreal Canadiens
  C.   The New York Rangers
  D.   The Chicago Blackhawks

2.3 Among the 35 NHLers on Team Canada, how many of them already had top-level international experience?

A. None
B. Two players
C. Four players
D. Six players

2.4 Why didn't Bobby Hull play for Team Canada at the Summit Series?

A. He was not invited
B. He was injured
C. He had to work on his farm
D. He was not an NHL player

2.5 Besides Bobby Hull, which other superstar didn't play for Team Canada?

A. Jean Beliveau
B. Gordie Howe
C. Bobby Orr
D. Gilbert Perreault

2.6 Which NHL goalie made a surprise visit to the Soviet dressing room just before Game 1 of the Summit Series?

A. Jacques Plante
B. Glenn Hall
C. Ken Dryden
D. Gump Worsley

2.7 What did the Soviet players write on their sticks for Game 1?

A. "Hammer and Sickle"
B. "Remember September"
C. "Montreal Surprise"
D. "Cold War"

2.8 In Game 2, who famously scored a highlight-reel goal for Team Canada, deking out two Soviet defenders in a one-man rush from his own end?

A. Bobby Clarke
B. Peter Mahovlich
C. Dennis Hull
D. Phil Esposito

2.9 Where did Team Canada claim its only victory in Canada?

  A. Montreal
  B. Toronto
  C. Winnipeg
  D. Vancouver

2.10 In what Canadian city did fans boo Team Canada?

  A. Vancouver
  B. Winnipeg
  C. Montreal
  D. Toronto

2.11 Which Team Canada member was seriously injured while playing against the Swedish nationals during the two-game hiatus in Stockholm before the Summit Series resumed in Moscow?

  A. Stan Mikita
  B. Don Awrey
  C. Wayne Cashman
  D. Mickey Redmond

2.12 What happened to Phil Esposito just before the start of Game 5?

  A. He slipped on the ice at the opening ceremonies
  B. He got into a fight in the dressing room
  C. He fired the puck at the opposition during warm-up
  D. He couldn't find his No. 7 jersey

2.13 How long did it take the Soviets to score four goals in their stunning comeback against Team Canada in Game 5?

  A. Under six minutes
  B. Between six and 12 minutes
  C. Between 12 and 18 minutes
  D. More than a period

2.14 How many players (at the time called "deserters") actually quit Team Canada mid-series to return home from the Soviet Union?

  A. Two players
  B. Four players
  C. Six players
  D. Eight players

2.15 Who did assistant coach John Ferguson call on to break the ankle of Valeri Kharlamov during Game 6?
- A. Rod Gilbert
- B. Serge Savard
- C. Pat Stapleton
- D. Bobby Clarke

2.16 What controversial action did the Soviets take that enraged Canadian officials prior to series-deciding Game 8?
- A. A lineup change
- B. A move to a new arena
- C. A referee switch
- D. An appeal for an international rule amendment

2.17 Who threatened to deliver a two-handed stick swing at referee Josef Kompalla and was subsequently thrown out of Game 8?
- A. Bobby Clarke
- B. Gary Bergman
- C. Jean-Paul Parise
- D. Guy Lapointe

2.18 During Game 8, what led series boss Alan Eagleson to jump out of his seat in order to reach the official timer's bench?
- A. A disputed penalty call
- B. A disruptive Soviet fan
- C. A malfunction in the arena clock
- D. The red light didn't go on to indicate a goal

2.19 How many seconds were left on the clock when Henderson scored the series-winning goal in Game 8?
- A. 14 seconds
- B. 24 seconds
- C. 34 seconds
- D. 44 seconds

2.20 While sitting on the bench, Paul Henderson called which player off of the ice, in order to play during the last minute of Game 8?
- A. Phil Esposito
- B. Peter Mahovlich

C. Yvan Cournoyer

D. Bill White

2.21 Which announcer said: "Henderson has scored for Canada"?

    A. Danny Gallivan

    B. Dick Irvin

    C. Foster Hewitt

    D. Bob Cole

2.22 What was the final goal count of the Summit Series?

    A. Team Canada 32–Soviet Union 31

    B. Team Canada 28–Soviet Union 27

    C. Soviet Union 28–Team Canada 27

    D. Soviet Union 32–Team Canada 31

2.23 Which Team Canada line was the only trio to remain together through all eight games of the Summit Series?

    A. Rod Gilbert, Jean Ratelle and Vic Hadfield

    B. Phil Esposito, Frank Mahovlich and Yvan Cournoyer

    C. Paul Henderson, Bobby Clarke and Ron Ellis

    D. No line survived intact for the entire series

2.24 How many players on Team Canada wore helmets?

    A. Only one player, Paul Henderson

    B. Two players

    C. Four players

    D. Five players

2.25 Through eight games of the Summit Series, the Soviets received 84 penalty minutes compared to how many by Team Canada?

    A. 67 minutes

    B. 87 minutes

    C. 127 minutes

    D. 147 minutes

2.26 Based on a shots-on-goal difference of 267 for Canada versus 227 for the Soviet Union, what was the final tally for shots-*at*-goal?

- A. Canada 481 versus Soviet Union 517
- B. Canada 499 versus Soviet Union 501
- C. Canada 501 versus Soviet Union 499
- D. Canada 517 versus Soviet Union 481

2.27 Which Summit Series player was named a game MVP most often?

- A. Phil Esposito
- B. Alexander Yakushev
- C. Paul Henderson
- D. Vladislav Tretiak

2.28 Who was the only player to participate in all of Team Canada's victories, plus the tie and none of its losses?

- A. Serge Savard
- B. Rod Gilbert
- C. Dennis Hull
- D. Bill Goldsworthy

2.29 Who recorded the most shots on net during the Summit Series?

- A. Yvan Cournoyer
- B. Boris Makhailov
- C. Alexander Maltsev
- D. Phil Esposito

2.30 Who has the puck that Paul Henderson shot for the winning goal?

- A. Paul Henderson
- B. A Soviet Ice Hockey Federation official
- C. The Hockey Hall of Fame
- D. Pat Stapleton

Summit Showdown

2.1 **A. One shot on net**

Only 30 seconds into hockey's most highly anticipated matchup ever, defenseman Gary Bergman wires a breakout pass to the line of Phil Esposito, Frank Mahovlich and Yvan Cournoyer. The trio swarms the Soviet net, as Mahovlich takes the first shot of the Series with a backhander that Vladislav Tretiak neatly kicks out. Esposito, parked as usual in front of the crease, bats the rebound out of the air and past a fallen Tretiak for the first goal of the historic tournament. The game was on.

2.2 **B. The Montreal Canadiens**

Canada's first team of professional players assembled for a major international event wasn't really a team at the beginning. Certainly, the 35 hand-picked players for the Summit Series were all born in Canada and played pro in the NHL. But when they arrived at training camp just two weeks before meeting the formidable Soviet national team, they were simply a collection of big NHL stars from opposing clubs. To many, including the players themselves, they weren't Team Canada at the start, they were still Phil Esposito of the Boston Bruins or Brad Park of the New York Rangers or Ken Dryden of the Montreal Canadiens. Further, during the four games in Canada, coach Harry Sinden's all-star ensemble played under his own self-imposed rule to get all 35 some ice time, a few new players being added to the starting lineup each game. After Game 4, with his Canadian team down 1–2–1, Sinden acknowledged some regret over his approach to ice time. As a result, it wasn't until Moscow that the team's core had been settled. And that cohesiveness, according to Yvan Cournoyer, was why Team Canada ultimately succeeded. "We got to play regularly with the same guys. And that's why we came back (to win)," said Cournoyer, one of six Montreal Canadiens on Team Canada. In all, among the 10 NHL clubs represented, the Canadiens contributed the most man-games with Cournoyer playing in all eight matches, followed by Pete Mahovlich (7), Guy Lapointe (7), Frank

Mahovlich (6), Serge Savard (5) and Ken Dryden (4). And unlike contributors from other NHL franchises, which had at least one or more players as spares on Team Canada, each of the six Habs played key roles in critical goals, including Cournoyer's go-ahead goal in Game 6 and tying goal in Game 8. Later, Serge Savard pointed out to Roy MacSkimming in *Cold War*, that, as a Montreal Canadien, playing against the Soviets' finesse game was a pleasure because it "was like playing against ourselves."

2.3 C. Four players

Canada went into the Summit Series with high expectations, but little in the way of firsthand experience against the Soviet national team. Among the very few who knew of the Soviets' skill and conditioning was head coach Harry Sinden, who had twice played for Canada internationally—as captain of the Whitby Dunlops at the 1958 World Championships and as a silver medalist during the 1960 Olympics. Canada defeated the Soviet Union at both events, but a generation of hockey had being played by 1972 and during that time the Soviets developed into a hockey dynamo, celebrating multiple world titles. Yet few players listened to Sinden, most believing in their own NHL invincibility. Ken Dryden was probably an exception, having backstopped Father Bauer's national team in 1969. Although no international experience could have prepared either team for what lay ahead at the Summit Series, three other players did play overseas prior to 1972: Red Berenson at the 1959 Worlds, Rod Seiling at the 1964 Olympics, and Brian Glennie at the 1968 Olympics. Interestingly, several members on Team Canada's roster played exhibition matches as juniors against the Soviets, including Bobby Orr, Serge Savard and Gilbert Perreault.

2.4 D. He was not an NHL player

Without overstating the case, it was considered a national emergency in Canada. Bobby Hull, multiple 50-goal scorer and owner of hockey's most explosive slapshot, was caught in the politics between rival leagues: the NHL, which had partnered with Hockey Canada to negotiate the landmark series, and the rebel World Hockey Association (WHA), the upstart circuit that was terrorizing the hockey establishment by signing NHLers to multi-million-dollar deals on teams going head-to-head in almost every

North American NHL market. Hull, the WHA's prize catch, would not be allowed to join Team Canada; or, as NHL president Clarence Campbell declared, if he did, the NHL would bar its players from competing in the tournament. Canadian fans were stunned by the ultimatum and "To Russia with Hull" signs began popping up everywhere, as the issue became a rallying cry across the country. Out of national interest, even Prime Minister Pierre Trudeau was asked to intervene. Hull called it "the most disappointing time" of his career and nicknamed Team Canada: "Team NHL," because of his exclusion to training camp. Bombastic Maple Leaf owner Harold Ballard may have said it best, declaring: "I don't care if Hull signed with a team in China. He's a Canadian and should be on the Canadian team." In all, four NHL defectors were scratched from coach Harry Sinden's original lineup, including Hull, Gerry Cheevers, Derek Sanderson and J.C. Tremblay.

2.5   C. Bobby Orr

Bobby Orr was Team Canada's number one spectator. Despite chronic knee ailments that prevented him from playing, Orr held out the hope that he might recover and travelled with the team throughout the series. He played the watchful spotter, relaying a tip early in the series, warning about the ineffectiveness of shot blocking against the Soviets. "The Russians don't even shoot from out there," Orr observed of the masterful cycling game executed by the Soviets deep in the offensive zone.

2.6   A. Jacques Plante

Before the series opener in Montreal, Vladislav Tretiak received an unusual visit from NHL veteran Jacques Plante, who, through a translator and with blackboard diagrams, instructed the young Soviet goalie on how to stop Canada's top snipers. Tretiak, whom Plante had tutored three years earlier when he was 17 and visiting Canada with his national junior team, said of the surprise encounter: "He showed me how the Canadians shot the puck. He talked about Cournoyer, Mahovlich, Esposito." Whatever possessed Plante, one of hockey's most learned goalies, to reveal such hockey secrets is not clear. Tretiak has his own theory: "I think he felt a little sorry for me. He didn't think I would do well." As it happened, the Soviets humiliated Canada 7–3, exposing Canada's biggest weakness—its lack of conditioning and game preparation, particularly in properly assessing Soviet strengths, such as Tretiak. After the loss, Pete Mahovlich unwittingly remarked that Tretiak had played him like he'd known him throughout his career, which leads to speculation on how Plante reacted to Canada's defeat that night? Was he smiling at his tutorial success, or regretful?

2.7 C. "Montreal Surprise"

It was Bobby Hull who called the Soviets "masters of deceit." And they were in fine Cold War espionage form for their preparation against Canada's best players at the Summit Series. While Canada was heavily criticized for not scouting their opponents properly, the Soviets gave nothing away before Game 1, as Canadian reserve goalie Eddie Johnston recounted in *The Days Canada Stood Still*. "I remember sitting in the Forum watching the Russians practise," said Johnston, "and it looked like it was going to be a blowout. They screwed around, nothing went right, they looked just awful. You couldn't help but wonder about this team." But all that changed when the Soviets stepped on the ice for real. Don Awrey remembers "Montreal Surprise" being painted on their sticks. "The name was all over them. It was like they knew what was going to happen," said Awrey. After the first period and a 2–2 score, the myth of Team Canada's might had vanished. "I went into the dressing room," said defenseman Bill White, "and everyone knew we'd been duped. I mean someone had made some serious scouting errors."

2.8 B. Peter Mahovlich

Few who saw it will ever forget the shorthanded goal that Peter Mahovlich scored in Game 2. With his team ahead 2–1 and the Soviets pressing hard in Canada's defensive zone, Phil Esposito blind-passed the puck off the boards and onto the stick of Mahovlich. From his own blue line, Mahovlich gathered steam up ice, deftly wheeled around Soviet defender Yevgeny Poladiev with a fake slapper and then made a forehand-backhand deke on Vladislav Tretiak that sent the Russian netminder sprawling and Maple Leaf Gardens into sheer pandemonium. It was all accomplished by pure hockey instinct. Mahovlich potted 288 goals in the NHL, but none were prettier or more inspired than his solo effort against the Soviets. Tretiak later recalled: "I remember that

One of the greatest plays and goals of the Summit Series: Peter Mahovlich puts the finishing touches on a superb solo rush and fakes out a sprawling Vladislav Tretiak in Game 2.

goal to this day. Each detail, each movement. And I still do not understand how he managed to score. Technically, I played it perfectly. And I did not make a mistake. Still, he got the puck past me and scored a very big goal. It was like magic." Today, many still consider Mahovlich's marker against Tretiak as one of the greatest goals ever scored in international hockey.

2.9   B. Toronto

After the debacle in Montreal, Team Canada regrouped to record their widest margin of victory of the series in Game 2. The 4–1 win at Maple Leafs Gardens would be their only Canadian triumph, but it brought the team their first taste of confidence after entering the event out of condition and ill-prepared for the Soviets' smart and swift-attack game. Retooling the team for the next match, coach Harry Sinden and assistant John Ferguson changed 40 percent of the first game's lineup, going with three forward lines and three pairs of defensemen. The Soviets' explosive assault and their knack for breaking a man up the middle, required forwards who could backcheck and rugged, mobile defensemen to keep their elusive opponents from winning the one-on-one battles in deep. Sinden's plan created new linemates, except the Henderson-Clarke-Ellis trio, which could score *and* check. Serge Savard, Bill White and Pat Stapleton, replaced shot-blocking rearguards Don Awrey and Rod Seiling; and Tony Esposito took Ken Dryden's spot in net. This wasn't the same Team Canada the Soviets played in Game 1, either in personnel or in attitude.

2.10   A. Vancouver

Almost nothing was predictable about the Summit Series. There were upsets and comebacks, political intrigue and drama, but would a hometown crowd ever boo its own team during such an important tournament? Unfortunately, that is what the humiliating 5–3 loss in Vancouver is remembered for, when spectators at Pacific Coliseum mercilessly booed Team Canada. The verbal abuse prompted Phil Esposito to give a stirring, heartfelt speech on national television, criticizing the boo-birds for their behaviour and lack of support. "I'm completely disappointed. I cannot believe it," Esposito said. "Every one of us guys—35 guys—we came out because we love our country. Not for any other reason. We came because we love Canada." It was an impassioned, sweat-soaked speech that moved the country and his besieged teammates. By the time they reached Moscow, the team had gelled and 10,000 telegrams arrived, wishing them luck in the series. After the Vancouver match, tournament organizer Alan Eagleson vowed to boycott the city in future series, a promise he kept until the Canada Cup in 1984, twelve years later.

2.11   C. Wayne Cashman

One of the biggest surprise selections for Canada's roster was scrapper Wayne Cashman. But coach Harry Sinden knew what he was getting in his Boston forward, who was one-third of the Cashman-Esposito-Hodge line that had powered Boston to two Stanley Cups. Sinden needed a pit bull in the corners, one who could deliver Bruins-style mucking in the Soviet end. It worked for two games as Cashman's physical presence helped turn Canada's play around with a win and tie in Game 2 and 3. He earned two assists in those matches but the referees were onto him and awarded him with 14 penalty minutes. In Game 4, he was replaced by tough-guy Bill Goldsworthy and never saw action again in the series. In the second exhibition game against Sweden's national team, Ulf Sterner jabbed his stick blade into Cashman's mouth and ripped a two-inch tear down the length of his tongue. The wound required 50 stitches inside his mouth, and kept Cashman from playing in the final four Moscow games.

2.12   A. He slipped on the ice at the opening ceremonies

During the player introductions at Moscow's Luzhniki Arena, Phil Esposito put his personal touch on the proceedings when he slipped on a flower stem on the ice and fell flat on his backside. Arena laughter followed cheers as Esposito played up the accidental tumble with his own chuckle on the ice, then a bow to the crowd that included many of the Soviet Union's highest-ranking politicians, such as Leonid Brezhnev and Alexei Kosygin. Goalie Vladislav Tretiak recalls: "You know if I had fallen down or any of the players we would be humiliated and confused. We would never have reacted the way Phil Esposito did, like an artist with such elegance."

2.13   A. Under six minutes

After building up an almost unbeatable 4–1 lead in the third period, Team Canada stopped skating on Moscow ice and gave up four goals, a credit to what backup goalie Eddie Johnston called the Soviets' great transitional game. "They could go from defense to offense, so quickly, and it caused us big problems. To put it bluntly, we really got burned," said Johnston. Canada's big lead evaporated in a span of under three minutes with three goals by Vyacheslav Anisin, Vladimir Shadrin and Alexander Gusev between 9:05 and 11:41. Vladimir Vikulov hammered out the four-goal third-period comeback with the capper at 14:46. All five goals in the Soviets' 5–4 upset came in the third frame on just 11 shots against Tony Esposito. Now, down 3–1–1 in the series, Canada's chances looked slim for their own comeback. But Paul Henderson, ever the optimist, saw something special happen to his team in that heartbreaking defeat: "We never gave up... We always had that feeling we were going to win... even after that game."

2.14 B. Four players

Among Team Canada's roster of 35 players coach Harry Sinden took overseas, at least a dozen knew they would see little or no ice time in Moscow. Most of those spares remained devoted to the core group's effort, but after learning who wouldn't be dressed in Game 5, Vic Hadfield and youngsters Jocelyn Guevremont and Rick Martin informed Sinden of their departure home. The troika was later joined by Gilbert Perreault, a surprise considering his play earned a goal and assist in the two previous matches. Sinden's reaction was predictable: "I didn't talk anyone into playing and I'm not going to talk anyone out of leaving."

2.15 D. Bobby Clarke

John Ferguson brooked few bounds in the no-holds-barred world of hockey. During his playing days, he was considered the NHL's undisputed heavyweight and the first true team policeman hired to protect smaller forwards. He helped guide Montreal to five Stanley Cups, including 1971's semi-final upset against Harry Sinden's vaunted Bruins. So when Sinden went looking for an assistant behind Team Canada's bench, he picked Ferguson, even though—according to Sinden—they had never met before off the ice and Fergie was without any coaching experience. However in Ferguson, Sinden found his match, a rugged finesse-and-fists battler who not only motivated players but also shared in his victory-at-any-cost philosophy. And against the Soviets, the price was a vicious premeditated two-hander across the ankle of their most dangerous player, Valeri Kharlamov. "Kharlamov had incredible skills," Ferguson later said in TV's *Summit on Ice* documentary. "He was hurting us all the time. I called Bobby Clarke over to the bench and I asked Bobby. I said 'Bobby, try to tap that ankle of his and try to break it. And we'll slow him down.' " Ferguson knew his bench very well. "Nobody else would do it [but Clarke]. That's the way *he* played the game too... No point in asking [Rod] Gilbert or Ellis or Henderson or even Espo. Clarke had the tenacity about him. He played to win," Ferguson concluded in *Cold War*. After Clarke hunted down Kharlamov, the Russian star was never the same. The slash put him out of Game 7, won by Canada, and limited him offensively throughout the final match. It may have been the edge

Ferguson sought with both teams so evenly matched and the whole world watching.

2.16 C. A referee switch

After Team Canada battled back to knot the series at 3–3–1 with a Game 7 victory, the Soviets announced a surprise referee change for Game 8 that would bring back West German officials Josef Kompalla and Franz Baader. The pair had worked with great incompetence in Game 6, meting out a disproportionately high penalty count of 31 minutes to the Canadians compared to the Soviets' four. Now, 24 hours before the biggest hockey showdown, an about-face on the selection of officials seriously threatened the entire series. Team Canada wanted Sweden's Uve Dahlberg and Czechoslovakia's Rudy Bata, who officiated Game 7. The next morning, on September 28, crucial negotiations were underway to settle if there would even be a final match. Finally, the suspense was broken with an agreement in the early afternoon: each side could pick one referee. But the Soviets applied one more twist to the drama, refusing to grant Canada its first choice of Dahlberg to referee. In the end, the Soviets got Kompalla and Team Canada went with Bata, a compromise by both parties that likely saved the series.

2.17 C. Jean-Paul Parise

Each successive game in the Summit Series ratcheted up the emotional intensity to create a war-like atmosphere. By Game 8, the pressure of winning led to several incidents, both on ice and behind the political scenes. Something had to blow. It came early in the eighth game after the Soviets had scored the game's opening goal with two Canadians—Bill White and Peter Mahovlich—sitting in the penalty box. Then, Jean-Paul Parise was handed a questionable interference penalty for banging into Alexander Maltsev. Parise was so enraged that he cursed at referee Josef Kompalla and slammed his stick on the ice, splintering it in the process. Kompalla, who wasn't even supposed to work the game (after his decidedly one-sided officiating in Game 6), immediately called an additional 10-minute misconduct for the transgression. With that, Parise lost it, and in one dramatic moment suddenly charged Kompalla and feigned whacking his stick at the cowering West German official. "I was going to hit him right over the head, but between starting and reaching where he was standing, I thought about what would happen, and I would probably have been banned for life. I had enough sense to pull back," Parise recalled in *The Days Canada Stood Still*. For that, the testy Parise received a game misconduct and watched the rest of the historic match from the sidelines. Then chairs, stools and towels were hurled over the boards from the Canadian bench. The pressure had been released and when play resumed, Team Canada found its composure and minutes later, with Soviet defenseman Evgeny Tsygankov in the box, Phil Esposito evened the score 1–1 on the ensuing power play. Parise led all players in penalties with 28 minutes through the series.

2.18   D. The red light didn't go on to indicate a goal

Paul Henderson's series-winning goal aside, the next most memorable event in the final match may have involved hockey czar Alan Eagleson, who scripted one of the more bizarre acts during a tournament remembered as much for the spectacle as for its political shenanigans. Midway through the third period, an overwrought Eagleson, obviously nerve-wracked from all the politics at play, clambered down rows of seats and past a wall of startled Soviet soldiers in an effort to reach the timer's bench. Eagleson's aim was to get Yvan Cournoyer's goal officially recorded after the red light failed to go on when the speedy winger deadlocked the game 5–5. But Eagleson's move was blocked by security forces, who literally dragged him away. Then, Peter Mahovlich, skating by, spotted his boss amid the brown uniforms and jumped the boards to free him from the scuffle. What came next gripped everyone as Mahovlich and his fellow rescuers paraded a disheveled Eagleson and others across the ice, their fists raised and middle digits extended, on their way to the safely zone of Team Canada's bench. Caught on television, the incident had diplomatic disaster written all over it. But the game continued, making it just another weird and irrational episode of the first-ever hockey summit.

2.19   C. 34 seconds

No one truly knew how evenly matched Team Canada and the Soviet Union were in 1972. Not the Soviets, who had done extensive research on their Canadian foes before coming over. Certainly not many on the Canadian side, all of whom had read the one-and-only scouting report, which famously and falsely cited Vladislav Tretiak's weak glove hand. And certainly not the few so-called "unpatriotic" mavericks, such as *Montreal Star* reporter John Robertson, who was calling for the Soviets to win the series, 6–2; or the lone wolf among prominent hockey thinkers, former NHL player Billy Harris, who coached the Swedish national team at the 1971 World Championships and 1972 Olympics. Harris may have been the true exception, calling for a 4-3-1 series win by the Soviets. No, it was not supposed to be a big series or so close; it was a novelty, not a serious competition. The Soviets, in their ill-fitting uniforms, were going to be easy pickings for Canada's top hockey arsenal. And though every Canadian player was nervous, they all wanted to give those upstart Russians a licking, and not leave it to Canada's out-matched amateur national teams at international events. But the Soviets arrived in superb condition playing a criss-cross skating game with intricate positional changes, meticulous puck control and a persistent regrouping in their own end, the likes of which North American players and fans had never seen. And it was that Soviet system, or, more precisely, the culture surrounding that regimented system, that led to the Soviets' downfall—just barely though, as the series unfolded. Because once Canada discovered their set patterns of play and broke down strategies with their own creative counterattack, the Soviets could be defeated. Meanwhile, the Soviets never adapted—as Canada did—to their opponent's game. They were robots of precision, rarely allowing for individual creativity, except for some sparkling play by Valeri Kharlamov. As many have said, the turning point in the series may have come in Game 5. Canada lost the match 5–4 but found something much more important: their momentum. Still, it took all eight games and until the score clock counted just 34 seconds before Paul Henderson threaded the puck through a narrow space between Tretiak's fallen body (yes, the glove side) and the left goalpost. Thirty-four seconds. Or about the time it's taken to read this account. As a result, 'hockey would change mightily. It proved that the skill gap was truly narrow, won by a single goal in the final minute of play. Unless, of course, you hold to defenseman Pat Stapleton's argument, that because of the wide disparity

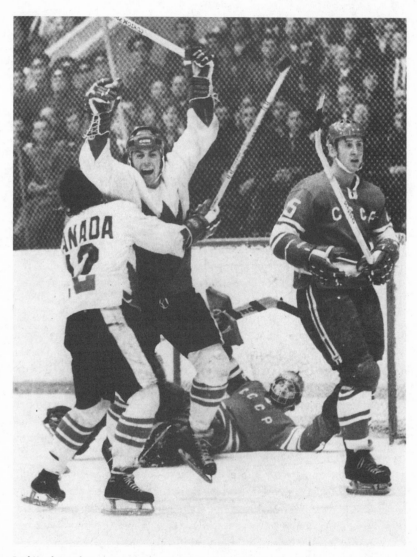

Paul Henderson leaps into Yvan Cournoyer's arms after scoring the winning goal in Game 8. Looking up from the blue paint is Vladislav Tretiak, as Soviet defender Yuri Liapkin stares off in disbelief. The iconic image is the most famous photograph in Canadian sports history.

in power plays favouring the Soviets, they "should've wiped the floor with us." Truthfully, between the Russians' puck movement and Canada's physical play, the Canadians learned as much about hockey from the series as the Soviets did. Before long, every world title at every tournament was up for grabs.

2.20   B. Peter Mahovlich
With less than a minute remaining and the series on the line in a 5–5 game, the Phil Esposito-Yvan Cournoyer-Pete Mahovlich line was close to ending its shift. Coach Harry Sinden decided he would finish with Clarke, Henderson and Ellis on the ice, but before the unit was dispatched, Henderson called three times on Mahovlich to come off. Mahovlich obliged and Henderson leaped over the boards, streaking into the Soviet zone to make history.

2.21   C. Foster Hewitt
Hockey's two most familiar phrases were both coined by Foster Hewitt, the legendary Maple Leaf broadcaster whose career began at the dawn of radio and who first uttered the soon-to-be ubiquitous "He shoots, he scores" sometime after going on air in February 1923. Almost 50 years later, Hewitt called the Summit Series and said it perfectly again with the timeless words: "Henderson has scored for Canada." In his lilted, high-pitched whine, Hewitt breathlessly called the action leading up to Paul Henderson's historic goal at 19:26 of the final period in Game 8. He said: "Cournoyer has it on that wing. Here's a shot—Henderson makes a wild stab for it and fell. Here's another shot! Right in front—They score!" And then came the quintet of words to describe the goal that would be talked about forever. Nearly everyone who saw or listened to the broadcast can recall where he or she was when that red light lit up behind a fallen Vladislav Tretiak. Then, Henderson stretched his arms high and leaped straight into Yvan Cournoyer's arms. It was as if, in that moment of pure joy, then in that next instant of relief and vindication, time stood still. It was a remarkable comeback against a Soviet club that had driven Team Canada to the brink of defeat. Working alongside Hewitt in the booth was colour man Brian Conacher.

2.22   D. Soviet Union 32–Team Canada 31
Canada may have won the Summit Series by a 4–3–1 margin, but the Soviets made every effort to remind fans that they actually

outscored their rivals in total goals, 32–31. The most lopsided score came in the first game when a total of 10 goals resulted in the surprising 7–3 Soviet victory. Canada stormed back to win Game 2 4–1, but settled for a 4–4 tie in Game 3 and a 5–3 loss in the fourth match. The remaining four games played in Moscow all ended with one-goal differences: 5–4 in favour of the Soviet Union in Game 5; and 3–2, 4–3 and 6–5 for Team Canada in the remaining games. Phil Esposito and Paul Henderson accounted for almost half of Canada's tallies, seven goals each. Vladislav Tretiak played all eight games, compared to his Canadian counterparts in net, Ken Dryden and Tony Esposito, who split the series four games apiece. Clearly, Tretiak was the busiest man between the pipes, facing 267 shots, or more than twice as many shots directed at either Canadian netminder. Against the world's best snipers, all three goalies notched save percentages below .900.

Summit Series Scoring

PLAYER	GP	GOALS	ASSISTS	POINTS	PIM
Phil Esposito	8	7	6	13	15
Alex Yakushev	8	7	4	11	4
Paul Henderson	8	7	3	10	4
Vladimir Shadrin	8	3	5	8	0
Valeri Kharlamov	7	3	4	7	16
Vladimir Petrov	8	3	4	7	10

Summit Series Goaltending

PLAYER	GP	MINS	GA	AVG.	SHOTS	SAVES	S%
Vladislav Tretiak	8	480	31	3.87	267	237	.884
Tony Esposito	4	240	13	3.25	110	97	.881
Ken Dryden	4	240	19	4.75	117	98	.837

2.23 C. Paul Henderson, Bobby Clarke and Ron Ellis

It was a scoring unit that no one really considered until coach Harry Sinden matched Toronto linemates Ron Ellis and Paul Henderson with that spunky "toothless" kid from Philadelphia. Even Henderson had his doubts about the young, diabetic Clarke, preferring a more reputable talent, such as Stan Mikita, to centre his line. But Clarke, the last player chosen to make Team Canada, came to camp determined to stay a regular on a squad of all-stars. Because he came without a reputation, Clarke knew he had to work harder and produce. On the Henderson-Clarke-Ellis line, he emerged with the same dominating force that would later win him three Hart Trophies as MVP in the NHL. The trio's two-way game, meshing offensive skill, checking ability and explosive speed, gave the Russians fits. They were creative, aggressive and competitive. Team Canada had Phil Esposito as scoring and inspirational leader, but Sinden's stroke of alchemical genius proved to be "the key to the series," according to assistant coach John Ferguson. The unit scored many of the series' big goals in the first five games with either Clarke or Ellis assisting on all of Henderson's goals; and Henderson or Ellis getting assists on Clarke's two markers. During the last three matches, Henderson wrote a script that even Hollywood wouldn't buy, by banging in three consecutive game-winners that dug Team Canada out of a very deep hole to capture the series and the imagination of hockey fans, to say nothing of restoring the nation's pride and self-esteem. Interestingly, none of those crucial game-winning goals authored by Henderson were assisted by linemates Ellis or Clarke.

2.24 **C. Four players**

While it was mandatory for every Soviet player to wear a helmet, only four Canadian players—Paul Henderson, Stan Mikita, Bill Goldsworthy and Red Berenson—did not play bareheaded. Few NHLers wore any headgear at the time, but it was fortunate for Canada that Henderson did. Shortly after he made it 3-0 in Game 5, the speedy winger was spun around by a Soviet defender going full bore to the net. He crashed heavily, back first, into the end boards and was knocked out cold. It took three ammonia packs from trainer Joe Sgro's medical kit to revive him after the nasty spill. Henderson shook off the cobwebs and returned in the third period despite doctor's pleas to sit out the game. On his very next shift, he scored a goal. Without the helmet, Henderson could have been lost for the series, a result that would have broken up Canada's most productive scoring unit.

2.25 D. 147 minutes

Because Canada and the Soviet Union each have their own distinct hockey organizations, culture and styles of play, when they first faced off in 1972, each side had to agree on the officiating. And while subtle differences existed between the international and NHL rule books, the larger question to settle was which referee system to use. It was decided that the two-man approach, using European referees, would be in play for the eight-game series, with each team picking the referees for alternate games. It was a concession by Canada that got the Soviets into the series. But hockey politics undoubtedly led to some bias in officiating when the teams got to Moscow and Team Canada narrowed the Soviets' series lead after winning Game 6. At that point, with what was at stake between the two hockey superpowers, the issue of choosing officials sharpened and became a potential advantage neither side could ignore. It led not only to backroom power plays between organizers but scores of penalties, mostly against Team Canada, who were assessed 105 minutes versus 48 for the Soviet team in the four matches at Luzhniki Arena. Perhaps the most startling stat was the man-advantage situations overall: the Soviets had 38 compared to 23 for the Canadians.

Summit Series In The Box

	CANADA	SOVIET UNION
Man-Advantages	23	38
Power-Play Goals	2	9
Shorthanded Goals	1	3
Penalty Minutes	147	84

2.26 A. Canada 481 versus Soviet Union 517

These numbers might appear odd based on their playing styles, with the Soviets' meticulously executed cycling game, where a shot was only taken when a real chance of scoring existed, versus the Canadians' up-and-down-the-lanes, then dump-and-chase method, but Canada had greater likelihood of an attempted shot resulting in an actual shot on goal. Team Canada fired 481 shots in the vicinity of Vladislav Tretiak, which produced 267 shots on goal. Meanwhile, the Soviets attempted 517 shots and 227 made it through to either Tony Esposito or Ken Dryden. So why the disconnect between the totals and the styles of play? Based on the stats alone, the Soviet shooters were either inaccurate in their aim or oddly unlucky with the posts and crossbar; or undone by Canada's superior shot-blocking unit. While Canada had better shot blockers, the Soviets rarely fired from far out; and they were, by no means, bad shots. Phil Esposito led all players with a shots-at-goal total of 89, or about 11 per game.

Summit Series Scoring Opportunities*

	GOALS	SHOTS ON	SHOTS AT	SHOTS ON %
Canada	31	267	481	56%
Soviet Union	32	227	517	44%

The shots-at-goal statistic includes actual shots on goal and shots that were blocked, hit the posts or crossbar, or went wide or high.

2.27 B. Alexander Yakushev

By his own account, the Summit Series was the turning point in the hockey career of Alexander Yakushev. Playing for Spartak Moscow, the second-best team in the Soviet Union after the Red Army club, Yakushev led his teammates in goals (7) and points (11) against Team Canada. For some, because of his size and offensive skills in the slot, he was the Soviet Phil Esposito. In fact, each netted a series high of seven goals. But unlike his Canadian counterpart, who wore his heart on his sleeve, Yakushev always had the same pensive, brooding expression, typical of the Soviets' seemingly dispassionate manner in competition. When asked about Yakushev, Esposito said there was no Russian player of the same skill level. In all four games in Moscow, Yakushev was chosen as MVP of the Soviet team, surpassing Esposito and Henderson, each with three MVP nods during the series. Yakushev also received the award for best forward in the series, while Brad Park was named top defenseman.

2.28 A. Serge Savard

As it worked out, Serge Savard couldn't have come up with more timely injuries, if there is such a thing in sports. An uncertain starter in Game 1's lineup due to a leg injury, Savard missed the

7–3 loss in Montreal, but played in Game 2's win in Toronto and Game 3's tie in Winnipeg. Then, at practice before the fourth game, a Red Berenson shot cracked his ankle, which sidelined him for the 5–3 defeat in Vancouver. As much as Team Canada needed his rugged mobility back on the blue line against the Soviet's swift transition game, Savard only became available after Game 5's 5–4 loss in Moscow. He returned for the remainder of the series, all one-goal victories for Team Canada. But Savard's distinction is unique not only among his teammates. Indeed, even among Soviet players, he alone can say he played in all his team's wins and the tie, while missing each of its losses. Interestingly, despite this achievement, the injury-plagued Savard managed a plus-minus of -1, only fifth best among eight rearguards on Team Canada.

2.29 D. Phil Esposito

Considering he still owns the NHL record for most shots in one season, it's not surprising that Phil Esposito not only led all shooters in the eight-game Summit Series, but almost doubled the next highest count by a Team Canada member and bested the top Soviet by 20 shots. Esposito was just coming off two record-setting NHL seasons of 550 and 426 shots. He was the triggerman with the fastest release and because of his size, he became this immovable force in the crease, a force that revolutionized the craft of scoring by parking himself in the slot. In the Summit Series, Esposito recorded 52 shots on goal, easily topping Alexander Maltsev's 32 shots and Paul Henderson's 28. Based on a team total of 267 shots, Esposito is responsible for firing every fifth shot by Canada.

2.30 D. Pat Stapleton

For almost 20 years nobody knew the whereabouts of hockey's most celebrated puck, the one Paul Henderson famously slipped behind Vladislav Tretiak on September 28, 1972. The more the question was asked, the more elusive the answer. Then, in 1992, sports columnist Jim Kernaghan of the *London Free Press* hooked up with defenseman Pat Stapleton for a story on the series' anniversary. Stapleton acknowledged he scooped up the puck and slipped it into his glove after the final whistle, but wouldn't confirm its true hiding place. Later, in a November 2000 story, he and Bill White claimed it was in the other's possession. "I always tell people I gave it to Bill White, and they can bother him," said Stapleton to the Canadian Press. "He's just trying to throw everybody off the trail," White countered, believing that Stapleton had it hidden in a safety deposit box. Other stories suggested it was in a box with a lot of pucks in Stapleton's garage or barn. So why all the secrecy? "Once we disclose where it is, the mystery is gone and I've got nothing to talk about," said Stapleton. Finally, on November 14, 2008, Stapleton solved the missing puck puzzle when he brought the fabled rubber out of hiding after 36 years and dropped it in a ceremonial faceoff prior to the start of a Junior B game between the Sarnia Legionnaires and St. Thomas Stars at Sarnia Arena. Stapleton, who played for the Legionnaires in 1958, was there to participate in a banner-raising ceremony in honour of Tommy Norris, the Sarnia manager who Stapleton credits with helping him make the pro ranks. Stapleton still won't reveal where he keeps it, nor what his eventual plans are, which is fine with Henderson, since it's a question of finders-keepers: "He (Stapleton) had the foresight to pick it up and see the value of it later down the road... Patty has it and it's his prerogative to do what he wants with it." And what does the prize look like? "It's just plain black, but it's marked," said Stapleton.

··· GAME 2 ···
Summit Series Sayings

DURING THE CLIMACTIC FINALE of Game 8 in the Summit Series, when organizer Alan Eagleson was rescued from the clutches of security forces by members of Team Canada, Bill Goldsworthy recalled: "In marched the Red Army surrounding the entire rink. Taking our position back on the bench, I turned to Wayne Cashman and said, "Well, how do you feel about spending the rest of your life in Siberia?" In this game, match the players below and their quotations.

Solutions are on page 138

Anatoli Tarasov	Serge Savard	Alan Eagleson
Phil Esposito	Pete Mahovlich	Valeri Kharlamov
Alexander Gusev	Viktor Kuzkin	Yuri Liapkin

1. _____ "The Canadians battled with the ferocity and intensity of a cornered animal."

2. _____ "I was a member of nine Stanley Cup teams, but this was the greatest experience of my career."

3. _____ "I thought I had one of the hardest slapshots in the world. When I arrived in Montreal, I discovered that almost every Canadian's shot was at least as hard as mine."

4. _____ "It was a war—our society versus theirs."

5. _____ "Nothing compared to the goal I scored in the second game of the series. In retrospect, I didn't deserve to be there in the series, but I went with 35 other guys ready to play and work hard. It all paid off."

6. _____ "It turned out to be my worst nightmare. Now, all of these years later everyone knows that Paul Henderson scored when Yuri Liapkin gave up the puck."

7. _____ "As captain, my job was to inspire my teammates both on and off the ice. But in this series that wasn't necessary."

8. _____ "I am convinced that Bobby Clarke was given the job of taking me out of the game. Sometimes I thought it was his only goal. I looked into his angry eyes, saw his stick, which he wielded like a sword, and didn't understand what he was doing. It had nothing to do with hockey."

9. _____ "We were all convinced we would win it eight straight. All we had to do was show up."

3

AN IDEAL OF GREATNESS

INTERNATIONAL HOCKEY'S EVOLUTION FROM amateur competition based in Europe to NHL involvement at the Olympics can be traced to several key events, none more important than the Canada Cup and its successor the World Cup of Hockey. These two tournaments finally brought together all of the world's best players and ultimately led to a greater NHL presence both at the World Championships and on Olympic ice. From 1976 to 2004, the Canada Cup and the World Cup of Hockey represented the true ideal of greatness to determine world champion. What evolved was a new generation of game as North American and European styles merged and parity among competing nations brought the level of international play up to standards rivaling Canadian and Soviet hockey.

Answers are on page 55

3.1   In which Canada Cup did opposing players first exchange their jerseys on ice after the series' final game?
    A. The 1976 Canada Cup
    B. The 1981 Canada Cup
    C. The 1987 Canada Cup
    D. The 1991 Canada Cup

3.2   Who scored the game-winning goal in overtime to defeat Czechoslovakia at the inaugural Canada Cup in 1976?
    A. Denis Potvin
    B. Darryl Sittler
    C. Guy Lafleur
    D. Bill Barber

3.3 Bobby Orr was voted MVP of the 1976 Canada Cup but, oddly, he was not voted MVP for Team Canada. Who won that honour?

A. Rogatien Vachon
B. Guy Lafleur
C. Darryl Sittler
D. Bobby Clarke

3.4 Which Canada Cup(s) did the Soviets win?

A. 1981
B. 1984
C. 1987
D. 1991

3.5 How is Canadian citizen George Smith linked to the 1981 Canada Cup?

A. He represented nickel giant Inco, who made the trophy
B. He smuggled the trophy out of Canada
C. He organized to make a replica trophy for the Soviets
D. He secretly etched his children's names on the trophy base

3.6 Which Canadian-born player suited up for USA at the 1981 Canada Cup?

A. Brian Engblom
B. Bryan Trottier
C. Bobby Hull
D. Tony Esposito

3.7 How many members of the Edmonton Oilers played for the Glen Sather-coached Canadian team at the 1984 Canada Cup?

A. Four Oiler players
B. Six Oiler players
C. Eight Oiler players
D. 10 Oiler players

3.8 Mike Bossy scored the overtime thriller against the Soviet Union during semi-final play at the 1984 Canada Cup, but which defenseman is responsible for the famous turnover on a Soviet odd-man rush in Canada's zone that led to Bossy's goal?

A. Kevin Lowe
B. Ray Bourque

C. Paul Coffey

D. Doug Wilson

3.9 **Who was named series MVP at the 1984 Canada Cup?**

A. Mike Bossy

B. John Tonelli

C. Wayne Gretzky

D. Michel Goulet

3.10 **What was the final score in all three games of the 1987 Canada Cup finals between Canada and the Soviet Union?**

A. 3–2

B. 4–3

C. 5–4

D. 6–5

3.11 **Who assisted on Mario Lemieux's famous series winner in 1987?**

A. Paul Coffey

B. Larry Murphy

C. Wayne Gretzky

D. Lemieux's goal went unassisted

3.12 **Whose cross-check on Wayne Gretzky during the 1991 Canada Cup caused the NHL to change its rules and assess an automatic game-misconduct to anyone who hits from behind?**

A. Gary Suter of USA

B. Viacheslav Fetisov of the Soviet Union

C. Chris Chelios of USA

D. Ulf Samuelsson of Sweden

3.13 **Which veteran NHL superstar did not play in any of the five Canada Cup series held between 1976 and 1991?**

A. Steve Yzerman

B. Dominik Hasek

C. Brian Leetch

D. Brett Hull

3.14 How much NHL experience did Eric Lindros have when he played in the 1991 Canada Cup?
- A. 80 NHL games
- B. 40 NHL games
- C. 20 NHL games
- D. None, Lindros was still in junior hockey

3.15 The US team dedicated their play in the 1991 Canada Cup to which individual or group?
- A. The US Olympic team of 1960
- B. The US troops in the 1991 Gulf War
- C. Their ailing coach, Bob Johnson
- D. The famed US Olympic team of 1980

3.16 Team Canada went undefeated in only one Canada Cup. Which one?
- A. 1976
- B. 1984
- C. 1987
- D. 1991

3.17 In the best-of-three finals against Canada at the 1996 World Cup of Hockey, USA won by which identical scores in both their victories?
- A. 3–2
- B. 4–2
- C. 5–2
- D. 6–2

3.18 Who scored USA's winning goal at the World Cup of Hockey in 1996?
- A. Brett Hull
- B. Tony Amonte
- C. Derian Hatcher
- D. John LeClair

3.19 In the first game of the 2004 World Cup of Hockey, Canada wore replica jerseys to celebrate which past Olympic champions?
- A. The 1920 Winnipeg Falcons
- B. The 1948 RCAF Flyers

C. The 1952 Edmonton Mercurys

D. Team Canada from the 2002 Olympics

3.20 **Which two teams played in the finals of the 2004 World Cup of Hockey?**

A. USA versus Finland

X B. Finland versus Canada

C. Canada versus Sweden

D. Sweden versus USA

3.21 **Who was named tournament MVP of the 2004 World Cup of Hockey?**

A. Martin Brodeur of Canada

B. Keith Tkachuk of USA

C. Fredrik Modin of Finland

X D. Vincent Lecavalier of Canada

· · · · · **ANSWERS** · · · ·

An Ideal of Greatness

3.1 **A. The 1976 Canada Cup**

It was an emotional moment few will forget. But who initiated the impromptu sweater exchange between Czechoslovak and Canadian players remains a mystery. Most fingers point to Peter Mahovlich, who later joked, "I took my sweater off after the final and gave it to a Czech player. Everyone followed suit. Still to this day, guys on our team tease me about that. They wanted to keep their sweaters." Others credit a group of Czechs, who, after the ceremonial handshakes, corralled series MVP Bobby Orr, slapping him on the back and tugging at their own sweaters. In one sponta-neous act of true sportsmanship, players swapped team jerseys. Bob Gainey slipped on Frantisek Pospisil's No. 7; Rogatien Vachon traded No.1s with Vladimir Dzurilla; and Darryl Sittler gave up his No. 27 to get Bohuslav Ebermann's No. 25. Bobby Clarke wasn't so fortunate. In the switch he was left without a Czech jersey and instead draped himself in the Canadian flag. Which lucky soul got Orr's No. 4 is unknown, although Orr donned Oldrich Machac's No. 4 in the swap. Today, Orr's other Canada Cup jersey (his red one) sits in the BC Sports Hall of Fame and Museum in Vancouver. Orr's father gave the jersey to cancer treatment activist Terry Fox on his heroic Marathon of Hope run across Canada.

3.2 B. Darryl Sittler

While Bobby Orr dominated both the play and the headlines as tournament MVP, the other Canadian hero of the 1976 Canada Cup was Darryl Sittler. The best-on-best series featured the finest players from the top six hockey nations, competing in what would become the first truly global hockey event, unlike the Olympics or World Championships at that time which did not include professional players. Teams played a round robin series followed by a best-of-three finals between the two squads with the highest point totals. In the finals' first match, Canada smothered defending world champion Czechoslovakia 6–0 on two goals by Orr, who was hobbled by knee problems so severe he played almost literally on one leg. The pressure on the Czechs to win Game 2 pushed the contest into overtime after each team had battled back with tying and go-ahead goals in the third period. In the extra session, tied at 4–4, Canada had two goals disallowed, one by Guy Lafleur after the net was deliberately displaced by the Czechs and the second by Guy Lapointe that came one-tenth of a second after the buzzer sounded to switch ends at the 10-minute mark. As the teams changed sides, assistant coach Don Cherry suggested that any player in alone against goalie Vladimir Dzurilla should try hesitating before shooting and "Let Dzurilla come out. Then try to step around the guy." A little more than a minute later Sittler streaked in past defenseman Jiri Bubla and faked a slapshot on Dzurilla that forced him to commit beyond his crease. Sittler took two more strides to the outside of the Czech netminder and smartly tucked the puck into the open net to give Canada the 5–4 victory. Canada had won the first true international best-on-best event.

3.3 A. Rogatien Vachon

Even with a bum knee, skating against the world's greatest players, Bobby Orr was still the best man on the ice at the 1976 Canada Cup. He scored a tournament-high nine points to win the MVP title, although some say he was a sentimental choice over

Rogatien Vachon, who was voted by Canadian team members as the squad's most valuable player. Vachon, a last-minute invitee to the series, may have had the dream team of blueliners in Orr, Denis Potvin and the Montreal Canadiens' "Big Three" of Larry Robinson, Serge Savard and Guy Lapointe, but of the 168 shots that found their way through on net, only 10 turned into goals, adding up to a stellar save percentage of .940 for Vachon. His spectacular play earned him every start of the series and won his team the inaugural Canada Cup. Still, he couldn't hide his disappointment over Orr being chosen series MVP. "I have to be honest. I thought I deserved the big award. Everyone said I would get it and I was disappointed when I did not," said Vachon.

3.4   A. 1981

Unlike the other four Canada Cups, the second edition of the tournament in 1981 featured a one-game, winner-takes-all final instead of the typical best-of-three format to determine world champion. After a preliminary round robin between the six teams, the four top clubs paired off for a one-game semi-final. In this series Canada beat USA 4–1 and the Soviets knocked out Czechoslovakia by the same score. This set up the one-game showdown for the championship between international hockey's greatest rivals, Canada versus the Soviet Union. In their first clash of the tourney, a meaningless 7–3 victory by Canada during the preliminary round, many felt that the Soviets under-played their true game in order to mislead Canada in case of a rematch in the final. Coach Viktor Tikhonov dressed backup goaltender Vladimir Myshkin instead of the great Vladislav Tretiak and said this about the loss: "The Canadians were superior to us when it came to guts and courage... My players reminded me of a boxer who comes into a ring with the notion in his mind that he's going to get beat up," said Tikhonov. While each team featured skill and speed to burn at both ends and seemed evenly matched with a strong contingent of young players anchored by veterans, the final game was a disaster for Canada as they were lit-up 8–1. Tretiak was back in net and stunted Canada's mightiest firepower in Guy Lafleur, Gilbert Perreault, Mike Bossy and a 21-year old Wayne Gretzky. Although the game was closer than the lopsided score, it was the worst defeat in Canadian hockey history. The main scapegoat for Canada's disgrace was goalie Mike Liut, who gave up five goals in the third period. Despite being a top NHLer during the 1980s, he was never invited back to the Canada Cup. "That's a game I'm going to have to live with for the rest of my life," said Liut. "That's just the way it is."

3.5   C. He organized to make a replica trophy for the Soviets
Cloak-and-dagger drama is one of international hockey's specialties, but rarely has it been a part of the world game on Canadian soil. That is until Manitoba's George Smith tried to do the right thing after Canada's stinging 8–1 defeat at the hands of the Soviet Union in the final game of 1981's Canada Cup. Like most Canadians, Smith watched Prime Minister Pierre Trudeau congratulate the Soviets and hand over the Canada Cup to captain Valeri Vasiliev at centre ice of the Montreal Forum. But when tournament organizer Alan Eagleson showed up with Montreal police in the Soviet dressing room after the game and snatched the trophy back, on the pretext that the hardware wasn't supposed to leave Canada, the Manitoba trucker decided to make it right. As Smith reasoned, the Soviets had won fair and square, and Eagleson's display of poor sportsmanship was a national embarrassment. He took his cause to the media and soon the donations poured in for Smith to make a duplicate Canada Cup for the Soviets. He received about 32,000 letters of encouragement, each containing a Canadian $1 bill. The story took another surprise turn when Smith donated much of the money to local amateur sports after a foundry heard of Smith's plea and promised to forge the trophy for free. None of this made a bitter Eagleson or Hockey Canada too happy. "They called the RCMP and CSIS [Canada's spy agency] and started harassing us," said Smith, who had undercover cops outside his office for several days. So Smith called up boyhood friend Ed Schreyer, who just happened to be Canada's Governor General at the time. Within 24 hours the agents were gone and soon after, Smith's Cup reproduction was presented to grateful Soviet ambassador at a public ceremony in Winnipeg. Today, the replica trophy is at the Russian Hockey Federation headquarters in Moscow, for everyone to see.

3.6   D. Tony Esposito

A handful of players suited up for adopted countries during the five Canada Cup series, including Canadian-born Tony Esposito for USA in 1981 and Czechoslovak Peter Stastny for Canada in 1984. For the 1981 Canada Cup, American general manager Lou Nanne had a few goalies on his radar, including Paul Skidmore and 1980 Olympic hero Jim Craig, but instead convinced Esposito, who had lived in Chicago for years, to get his American citizenship just prior to the tournament. Even at 38 years old, "Tony O" gave USA instant credibility between the pipes and the chance to steal a few wins with his extensive international experience. Unfortunately, the Americans, coached by the legendary Bob Johnson and led by Neal Broten, Dave Christian and blueliners Rod Langway and Mark Howe, couldn't win more than two games and finished the tournament in fourth place. Meanwhile, Stastny is interesting because he is the only player to represent three countries—Czechoslovakia, Canada and Slovakia—in international hockey, each at the highest levels of competition. He played in two Olympics, five World Championships and a pair of Canada Cups, first with Czechoslovakia, prior to his defection from that country to the NHL in 1980; then as a member of Team Canada after receiving Canadian citizenship for the 1984 Canada Cup; and, finally, with his true home country of Slovakia during the early 1990s, following the political breakup of Czechoslovakia. His play for Canada created an unusual challenge for Czechoslovak TV announcers during the 1984 Canada Cup. They considered his inclusion on the Canadian team a provocation. For political reasons, whenever he had the puck, they weren't permitted to say his name. Although Czechoslovakians at home knew his uniform number and could read the name on his Canadian jersey, whenever Stastny had the puck, Czech commentators remained silent and after his goal against his former Czech team in a 7–2 Canada win on September 8, they were only allowed to say: "Goal by number 26 for Canada."

3.7   C. Eight Oiler players

Glen Sather didn't have to look much beyond the royal blue and copper "oil drop" crest of the Stanley Cup champion Oilers to fill up his Canada Cup roster in 1984. The architect of that era's next great NHL dynasty, Sather, stocked one third of Team Canada or "Team Oiler," as media critics named them, with Wayne Gretzky, Mark Messier, Paul Coffey, Glenn Anderson, Kevin Lowe, Randy Gregg, Charlie Huddy and Grant Fuhr. He also had familiar personnel behind the bench in Edmonton assistant coaches John Muckler and Ted Green. There was no doubt Sather built his Canadian team on the Oilers' freewheeling, attack-oriented style of play, but with their youth, speed and firepower he added experience and, well, more blinding firepower in mobile defensemen such as Larry Robinson, Ray Bourque and Doug Wilson. Up front, Sather iced scoring aces Mike Gartner and Michel Goulet, as well as four members of the New York Islanders, the Oilers chief NHL adversaries in two previous Stanley Cup final. Neither group of players in the Oilers-Isles rivalry liked each other much, even admitting so in player meetings. This tension led to a disappointing 2–2–1 record for fourth-place Canada in the round robin. Much was made of their feud and the subsequent struggle to gel as a team, but in the semi-final showdown against the Soviets, their combination gave the 1984 Canada Cup its most compelling moment and redeemed Team Canada on home turf.

3.8 C. Paul Coffey

Despite Paul Coffey's long and distinguished career as an NHLer, his most famous play probably came in international hockey. In fact, in all of the titanic clashes between the Soviet Union and Canada, few individual efforts have altered the course of a championship more dramatically. During 1984's preliminary round Canada had struggled, winning only two of five games and losing their most important match-up, a 6–3 defeat to the archrival Soviets. The famed Soviet national team was peerless since being embarrassed by the Americans at the 1980 Olympics. After that humiliation, the Big Red Machine retooled with the "KLM Line" of Vladimir Krutov, Igor Larionov and Sergei Makarov and notched three straight World Championships in 1981, 1982 and 1983, the 1981 Canada Cup and the 1984 Olympics. Their blitzkrieg continued through the 1984 round robin with five victories and a stifling 22–7 goal differential against their opponents. The semi-final showdown against the Canadians was considered by many to be for the championship since the winner would play weaker Sweden in the best-of-three finals. And Team Canada looked vulnerable, playing hot and cold throughout the series. But revenge was Canada's weapon du jour against the Soviet advance. "They beat us in '81 and we spent three years hearing they were the best in the world," said Wayne Gretzky. Canada's inspired play showed on the shot clock with a 35–20 advantage, but the score was deadlocked 2–2 after three periods. Then, 12 minutes into overtime, the Soviets stormed into the Canadian zone with a deadly two-on-one break, spearheaded by Vladimir Kovin, who had the puck and Mikhail Varnakov on his wing. Because of his great offensive skills, Paul Coffey was seldom called on as the last blueliner in his defensive zone. But there he was facing down two of the most skilled Soviet forwards with only goalie Pete Peeters between him and a potential Canada Cup loss. Still, Coffey read Kovin's saucer pass to Varnakov perfectly and executed a textbook defensive maneuver by lifting his stick at the precise moment to intercept the puck. He quickly counterattacked and moved the play back into the Soviet zone, stymieing the Soviet's near-lethal strike. John Tonelli's tenacious work in deep brought the puck back out to Coffey, who was now in his more familiar position on the point. Coffey blasted a shot, which Mike Bossy redirected into the net behind Soviet netminder Vladimir Myshkin. Canada won 3–2 and in the coming days avenged their Canada Cup disgrace of 1981 by taking two straight games from Sweden in the finals to reclaim the Canada Cup.

3.9   B. John Tonelli

The high-risk, high-reward tactics of Glen Sather's Canadian squad at the 1984 Canada Cup borrowed heavily from the firewagon hockey of the Edmonton Oilers and adapted it to the international game. Thankfully for Team Canada, Sather had the good sense to mix his core skill group with some New York Islander grit in Brent Sutter, Bob Bourne and John Tonelli. Along with Isles sniper Mike Bossy, the foursome made the greatest impact in the most important game of the tournament, playing clutch hockey in their semi-final matchup against the unbeaten Soviets. Their tenacious play every shift and for every inch of territory in the corners, along the boards and on open ice motivated their teammates while intimidating the opposition. The Islanders had learned how to win NHL titles after four straight Stanley Cups, 1980 to 1983. And they had given the bold and brash Oilers about 10 years of experience in two weeks during playoff action in 1983 when the Islanders swept the Cup final. "That's why they won and we lost," Gretzky later confessed. "They took more punishment than we did. They dove into more boards, stuck their faces in front of more pucks, threw their bodies into more pileups. They sacrificed everything they had." Now, the Islanders were again demonstrating the bruising art of winning. Tonelli and Bossy each had goals against the Soviets, with Coffey assisting on both, including the 3–2 overtime winner by Bossy. On Doug Wilson's marker, Gretzky and Bourne assisted. The Oiler-Islander combination finally clicked and Sather would have victory. But none of the big guns were named series MVP. It went to Tonelli, the bull on the ice who first turned down a Team Canada invitation to training camp. Why? He felt he wasn't good enough.

3.10 D. 6–5

The most dramatic and finest hockey ever staged may well be the epic final at the 1987 Canada Cup. It featured perhaps the strongest rosters ever assembled by Canada and the Soviet Union at a time when the two elite hockey nations possessed deep talent pools, with several key players in their prime. The Canadians were well seasoned with Stanley Cup–winning Oilers in Wayne Gretzky, Paul Coffey, Mark Messier and Grant Fuhr; Ray Bourque and Larry Murphy on the blue line; and the rising star of Mario Lemieux. The Soviets iced their explosive five-man unit of the "KLM Line" (Vladimir Krutov, Igor Larionov and Sergei Makarov) and defensemen Viacheslav Fetisov and Alexei Kasatonov. But deeper into both lineups, there were many other top-shelf snipers and talented grinders who, though less famous, were no less valuable in the war on ice. Moreover, the fierce hockey rivalry between the two countries had sharpened their skills to new levels since the historic Summit Series in 1972. Unlike at that event, where so much was unknown, now no one took anything for granted. Further, the Canadians' NHL-style of dump-chase-and-grind hockey and the Soviets' passing-and-speed game morphed over the years to include elements of the other. As a result, the teams couldn't have been more evenly matched or the games more tightly contested as all three games recorded identical 6–5 scores, which was the goal count in the monumental eighth game of 1972. In 1987's first game of the finals, the Soviets claimed victory on a goal by Alexander Semak after five minutes of overtime. In Game 2, the clubs battled through regulation time and another gruelling 30 extra minutes before Mario Lemieux redirected a Gretzky shot past Soviet goalie Evgeny Belosheikin to force a third game. In the winner-take-all match, Team Canada fell behind 3–0 and 4–2, but then rallied to take a 5–4 lead. They lost the lead again after the Soviets tied it at 12:21 on a third-period marker, again by Semak. With 1:26 remaining, Mario Lemieux potted the Canada Cup winning goal in the series' third consecutive 6–5 contest. Gretzky later remarked it was probably the best hockey he ever played.

3.11 C. Wayne Gretzky

When coach Mike Keenan finally caved to the tantalizing prospect of pairing the playmaking wizardry of Wayne Gretzky and the scoring virtuosity of Mario Lemieux at the 1987 Canada Cup, the result was, well, a big bang that produced the greatest tandem ever iced on the international stage. The pyrotechnics unleashed by the duo won the series for Canada, as each man led the tournament in their respective skills, and, more importantly, combined to score two game-winners in the best-of-three finals against the Soviets. What fans remember most from that series was Mario Lemieux's electrifying Cup-winning goal with under two minutes to play in the final game. The score was tied 5–5 and Dale Hawerchuk won a crucial faceoff in the Canadian end. Lemieux gathered up the loose puck and fed it to Gretzky. Hockey's greatest one-two combo broke down the left wing with only Soviet defender Igor Kravchuk back. Gretzky faked out Kravchuk by using Larry Murphy on the right wing as a decoy and slid the puck back to Lemieux, who was trailing on the play. Lemieux scoped the net for a split second as he flew through the faceoff circle then buried a wrister in the top corner behind Sergei Mylnikov's glove to give Canada some last-minute heroics in the 6–5 championship game. The goal for Lemieux, just 22 years old, was a turning point in his stellar career. "He [Gretzky] really showed me how to be a winner, how hard you have to work to become the number one player in the world," said Lemieux, who led all tournament scorers with 11

Wayne Gretzky and Mario Lemieux team up to score the most celebrated goal of the 1987 Canada Cup: the 6–5 Cup-winner against the Soviet Union in the dying moments of Game 3.

goals. Gretzky recorded three goals and 18 assists in nine games, the series' leading point-getter.

3.12 A. Gary Suter of USA

Gary Suter broke a lot of ground in the NHL with his controversial stick work in international hockey. On two occasions at the Canada Cup, in 1987 and again in 1991, he used his lumber to disable opponents, with some ugly results. In 1987, Suter whacked Soviet forward Andrei Lomakin across the face and received a five-minute major. While he continued to play in the tournament, the NHL, in an unusual move, suspended him for the first four games of the 1987–88 season, as well as the next six international contests that had NHL participation. Then, during Game 1 of the 1991 Canada Cup, he cross-checked Wayne Gretzky into the corner boards behind the US net. "I was a good four feet from the boards," said Gretzky. "I knew we were shorthanded and I wanted to make a play. Then, the first thing I knew my head was hitting the glass." Gretzky slumped to the ice in pain. No penalty was called on the play and even No. 99 later said that he didn't think Suter's hit was dirty. "It was a legal hit," claimed Suter. "I didn't try to hurt the greatest player in the world." Although he was able to leave the ice under his own power, Gretzky was sidelined for the rest of the series with back spasms. After the incident, he was dogged by chronic back pain and the condition eventually forced him to miss half of the 1992–93 season. Even though the check wasn't penalized, the NHL realized how close the hit had come to ending the career of hockey's premier talent. As a result, the league began assessing automatic game misconducts to any player who hit or pushed another player from behind.

3.13 A. Steve Yzerman
Although the five Canada Cups gave hockey fans a chance to see their favourite NHL players in world competition, inevitably, the overabundance of talent, particularly on Team Canada, led to a number of NHL stars with impeccable credentials being cut. In 1987, Canada could have sported a second national team after releasing Patrick Roy, Wendel Clark, Denis Savard, Scott Stevens, Cam Neely, Al MacInnis, Dino Ciccarelli and, perhaps the most perplexing cut of all, Steve Yzerman. In fact, Yzerman is probably the best player to be twice snubbed (although Savard ranks a close second with rebuffs in 1984 and 1987). Yzerman got the hook first in 1987 and, then, again in 1991, when coach Mike Keenan jettisoned the Detroit star after his milestone 51-goal season. The decision was as unpopular as a later decision by Marc Crawford who overlooked Mark Messier in favour of Rob Zamuner at the 1998 Olympics.

3.14 D. None, Lindros was still in junior hockey
Eric Lindros is the only Canadian team member to ever play in a Canada Cup tournament without NHL experience. The

wunderkind of Canadian junior hockey was just 18 years old when he was invited to training camp for the 1991 Canada Cup. Skilled beyond his years, he made the team because of his poise, physical play and scoring ability, a rare instance of a superstar wrapped in the body and mind-set of an enforcer. Lindros was Team Canada's biggest player at six-foot-four and 225 pounds and he took every opportunity to show he belonged and could excel at hockey's highest level. He scored three goals and five points in eight games, but it was his bruising style of play that left the biggest impression, especially on Swedish defenseman Ulf Samuelsson, whose tournament was cut short after a Lindros hit separated his shoulder; and Czech winger Martin Rucinsky, who suffered a broken collar bone in a thumping by the teenage phenom. No less an authority than Theo Fleury (whose credentials include the fight that started the infamous Punch-up in Piestany) said this about his Canada Cup teammate: "When he hits you, he can hurt you. No check that—he can kill you." The trail of broken bodies left in Lindros' wake during Canada Cup only raised his value for his NHL rights holder, the Quebec Nordiques. But Lindros refused to sign with Quebec after the 1991 draft, so he played with Canada's national team in 1991–92, winning a silver medal at the 1992 Albertville Olympics. Interestingly, despite his NHL fame, Lindros was far more successful as an amateur and pro in international play. Besides his silver at the 1992 Winter Games, he claimed two gold medals at the World Juniors in 1990 and 1991 and the 1991 Canada Cup championship, all of which came well before his first game as an NHL rookie with the Philadelphia Flyers. Lindros also won an Olympic gold medal in 2002.

3.15   C. Their ailing coach, Bob Johnson

More than just the US hockey team's leader, Bob Johnson was instrumental in the development of American hockey, both at the college level and in NHL play. When he suddenly fell ill and was diagnosed with two brain tumors just days before the 1991 Canada Cup round robin began, he was immediately admitted to a Pittsburgh hospital where surgery was performed to remove one tumor and radiation was applied to treat the other. Despite his hospitalization and grave state of health, "Badger Bob" remained a central figure on the team, sending messages of encouragement to the players throughout the tournament and even detailed game plans to assistant coach Tim Taylor. Johnson's influence was such that almost every player in his sphere could say their careers were affected in one way or another by his coaching. He became their inspiration and, ultimately, the fallen hero to whom the players dedicated the tournament. "We want to win this thing for Bob, for ourselves and for all of America," said Joey Mullen, just before USA's semi-final 7–3 victory against Finland. Teams have sometimes risen from disaster to championship through the inspiration of one individual, but few squads have ever displayed more purpose than the Americans playing for Johnson in 1991. And although they had arguably their deepest lineup in Canada Cup history and went on to lose the finals by scores of 4–1 and 4–2 against Canada, USA had finally arrived as an international hockey powerhouse, thanks in no small measure to their guiding light and inspirational leader, Bob Johnson.

3.16 D. 1991

Canada may not have won the 1991 championship as dramatically as the Canadian squad did in 1987's tournament, but, in many respects, they were a better balanced and more complete team, going undefeated throughout the series with a 6–0–2 record. It was the only time any team managed to play in a Canada Cup without a loss. And they did it without 1987's high-powered attack of Wayne Gretzky and Mario Lemieux, instead relying largely on their one go-to guy in Gretzky and a support cast of hard-nosed, two-way warriors such as Steve Larmer, Theo Fleury, Mark Messier and Rick Tocchet to compliment Bill Ranford between the pipes. Ranford started all eight games after preserving a 2–2 wakeup call against upstart Finland in the series' first contest. Then, in workmanlike fashion, the Canadians beat USA 6–3, Sweden 4–1, Czechoslovakia 6–2 and tied Russia 3–3 before blanking Sweden 4–0 in the do-or-die semi-final. Two consecutive victories in the best-of-three finals against a strong USA squad earned Team Canada its fourth Canada Cup and recognition as the only unbeaten club in tournament history. Overall, Ranford gave up just 14 goals in 8 games while facing 243 shots for an average of 30 shots per match. The muckers and bangers had done their job to keep the shot count down in a series where, for the first time, there was near-parity among all six competing nations. With a sizzling .939 save percentage, Ranford was named MVP of the Canada Cup, but, up front, he had the finest two-way team in the world.

3.17   C. 5–2

Although the Americans won Olympic gold in 1980, their emergence as a true hockey power came at the Canada Cup in 1991. They recorded consecutive losses in the best-of-three finals, but the fact that Canada's opposition that year was USA and not their archrival, the Soviet Union, was a major turning point in US hockey history. The nucleus of American players from that squad was now in its prime for the 1996 World Cup of Hockey. Not surprisingly, they were considered the favourites with a roster that would challenge Canada in the corners, along the boards and in front of the net, as coach Ron Wilson promised. Against the Canadians, the style of play would be decidedly North American, so Wilson deployed a power package of forwards in Keith Tkachuk, Bill Guerin and Adam Deadmarsh, all tough check-finishers to compliment the speed and offensive might of John LeClair, Pat Lafontaine, Mike Modano, Doug Weight and Brett Hull, one of two Canadian-born ex-pats (along with Deadmarsh) in the lineup. A first-class corps of blueliners included Brian Leetch, Derian and Kevin Hatcher, Phil Housley and Mathieu Schneider. This was a team as mean and tough as any in any tournament, but the star would prove to be goalie Mike Richter. After suffering a 4–3 overtime loss in Game 1 of the best-of-three finals, Richter stoned the Canadian squad time and again in the second and third matches, winning first star of each 5–2 victory. In Game 2's third period, with Canada down 3–1, Richter made 17 saves on 18 shots to secure the win and knot the series. Then, in the second frame of the third game, it was all Richter again, stemming a 22-shot barrage, except for a late-period wrist shot from Eric Lindros, low and to the far side. Team Canada had finally found a hole in Richter and tied the score 1–1 after blasting away unsuccessfully for 32 shots in two periods of play. The Abington, Pennsylvania native was the ultimate difference for USA, as each game was closely contested, with two empty net goals in Game 2 and another in Game 3 against the Canadians. It was America's first world title in 16 years, dating to the 1980 Olympics.

3.18 B. Tony Amonte

With less than three minutes remaining in the final game, Tony Amonte lifted a rebound from a Derian Hatcher point shot over Curtis Joseph to give USA a 3–2 lead against their northern rivals. Team Canada never recovered and the goal by the native of Hingham, Massachusetts stood up as the series clincher in USA's 5–2 victory. Surprisingly, the historic win generated little fanfare in Amonte's homeland. In established hockey markets it led the evening sports news, but in non-traditional markets the celebrations received very little attention and not a single word about Amonte's exploits appeared in the Hingham newspaper, evidence of how little impact the World Cup of Hockey had on the American consciousness. If his goal had been scored during the Olympics, it's likely Amonte would have become a household name.

3.19 A. The 1920 Winnipeg Falcons

In their opening game of 2004's eight-team tournament, Canada faced USA sporting a new look: instead of Hockey Canada's familiar logo (a red-and-black maple leaf with a silhouetted player), they donned vintage uniforms of those worn by the 1920 Winnipeg Falcons, the first Olympic gold medalists in hockey. It was the first time that most Canadians had heard of the champion Falcons, who received the tribute after more than 80 years of neglect. The 2004 squad's gold jerseys, with a wide black band and serrated red maple leaf lettered with "Canada," were true to the original in appearance, including a small Winnipeg Falcons shoulder patch. Only uniform numbers and player names were added to the replica sweaters, as the 1920 team likely had neither without such a tradition in place and a roster of just eight men. Their historic Olympic victory in 1920, including a 2–0 win against USA in the gold-medal round, inspired Team Canada in 2004, where they outshot the Americans 32–24 in the hard-hitting, face-paced first game. Canadian goalie Martin Brodeur and US counterpart Robert Esche duelled, with each making spectacular plays, but Canada prevailed against their old 1920 Olympic rivals by the slim margin of 2–1.

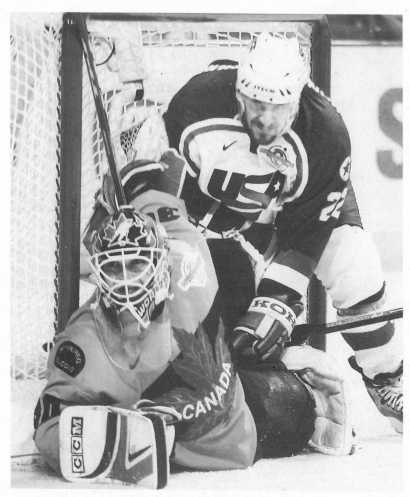

At the 2004 World Cup of Hockey, Team USA's Steve Konowalchuk slides into Canada's Martin Brodeur, who is wearing a replica sweater of the 1920 Winnipeg Falcons, the first Olympic titlists in hockey.

3.20 B. Finland versus Canada

After the preliminary rounds and quarter-final play, Finland squared off against USA and the Czech Republic faced Canada in the semi-finals, each vying to succeed the single-game knock-out for a berth in the championship game. Both contests featured tight, one-goal victories, as one of Canada's youngest international teams (12 players were under age 25) weathered a tense 4–3 overtime win; and a surprising strong Finnish squad squeaked by with just 12 shots on American goalie Robert Esche, who claimed "fluke" goals led to the 2–1 defeat of his defending World Cup champion USA team. While 2004 would be Canada's seventh consecutive tournament final, it was the first by Finland, a team that had won only one major title ever—the 1995 World Championships. Playing their defense-first game and skillfully capitalizing on opponent's mistakes throughout the event, the Finns entered the finals undefeated with four wins and one tie compared to Canada's unblemished mark of 5–0–0. Similar to previous matches, Canada came out flying but each time they scored, Finland responded, until Shane Doan potted the winner on a give-and-go with Joe Thornton just 34 seconds into the third period. It proved to be the turning point of the game. From there both teams played exciting, solid hockey, but Martin Brodeur took over and the Finns couldn't net the equalizer. Canada emerged with a 3–2 victory and the title as world champion again. The next day NHL commissioner Gary Bettman suspended league operations and the long-pending player lockout was underway. How long hockey would be gone was anyone's guess.

3.21 D. Vincent Lecavalier of Canada

Just three months after Vincent Lacavalier notched nine goals and seven assists in the Tampa Bay Lightning's 2004 Stanley Cup victory, the big centre was at it again, playing championship hockey with seven points in six games at the World Cup of Hockey. Lecavalier wasn't even an original selection for Canada but his Stanley Cup performance and an injury to Steve Yzerman landed him a spot in the lineup. And how fortunate that was for Canada. His most important goal came in the sudden-death semifinal match against the Czech Republic, when he scored the overtime winner that sent Canada to the finals against Finland. With the game knotted 3–3, Lecavalier took a pass from Ryan Smyth, shot, then roofed his own rebound from an almost impossible angle past Tomas Vokoun at 3:45 in the extra period. "After I missed my first shot, it went between my legs," Lecavalier said. "I knew I didn't have much time so I just turned around and shot it as quickly as I could. I knew I had to go high. With the angle I had, I got pretty lucky."

• • • GAME 3 • • •
Twist of Fate

BELIEVE IT: THE FIRST hockey club to represent Canada sporting the famous red maple leaf on their uniform was actually a team from Britain. They were known as the Oxford Canadians, a squad of Canadian students on scholarship at Oxford University who were widely regarded as the most dominant team in Europe before World War I. In this game, match the names below with their unique stories.

Solutions are on page 138

Serge Savard   Mike Buckna   Karil Yugorov

Bram van der Stok   Kim Martin   Frantisek and Zdenek Tikal

Vasily Tikhonov   Steve Konowalchuk

1. _____ The Canadian who became the father of Czech hockey.
2. _____ He gave away a friend's prized autographed hockey stick to Prime Minister Pierre Trudeau—as a prank.
3. _____ He was the Soviet public address announcer with a hidden past who was the voice at Moscow's Luzhniki Arena during the 1972 Summit Series.
4. _____ She was only 15 years old when she backstopped her country to Olympic bronze in 2002.
5. _____ They were twin brothers who faced off against each other while playing for different teams at the 1960 Olympics.
6. _____ The son of the Soviet Union's most famous coach, he became the first Russian-born head coach of a North American pro hockey team.
7. _____ He was the only NHLer born in the host city of the 2002 Olympics, Salt Lake City, yet he did not compete before home town fans at the event.
8. _____ He took part in the "Great Escape," one of the most famous Allied prisoner breakouts during World War II, after which a Hollywood feature film was made.

4

CHAMPIONS OF THE WORLD

THE NHL'S ANNUAL OUTDOOR Winter Classic has received nothing but rave reviews, but many fans are unaware that hockey's first major open-air game happened in, of all places, Moscow. More startling, the game took place prior to the democratization of Russia, in the communist Soviet Union. Sweden and the Soviets were playing for the gold medal in the 1957 World Championships at the Luzhniki Arena. With an arena seating capacity of just 14,000 and the national team vying for the championship, organizers moved the all-decisive game to the nearby Luzhniki soccer stadium to meet ticket demands. Unfortunately, the Soviets lost the world title in a 4–4 tie, but the 50,000 spectators in attendance set a still-standing international record. In this chapter, we take a seat at the World Championships.

Answers are on page 77

4.1　In what year did Canada first host the World Championships?
- A.　1978
- B.　1988
- C.　1998
- D.　2008

4.2　What is the record for most games appeared in by a player at the World Championships?
- A.　Less than 90 games
- B.　Between 90 and 110 games
- C.　Between 110 and 130 games
- D.　More than 130 games

4.3　Which senior amateur team from Canada won the 1961 World Championships?
- A.　The Whitby Dunlops
- B.　The Trail Smoke Eaters
- C.　The Penticton Vees
- D.　The Chatham Maroons

4.4 In what year did women first play for a gold medal at an IIHF World Championship?

    A. 1970

    B. 1980

    C. 1990

    D. 2000

4.5 Why did Czechoslovakia not defend their 1949 World Championship title at the next tournament in 1950?

    A. Team members were jailed as state traitors

    B. Team members died in a plane crash

    C. Team members were expelled from their country

    D. There were no World Championships in 1950

4.6 Which country's national team iced the so-called "Donald Duck Line" at the 1995 World Championships?

    A. USA

    B. Finland

    C. Canada

    D. Sweden

4.7 In what year did Canada withdraw from international hockey after a dispute over the use of amateur and professional players?

    A. 1950

    B. 1960

    C. 1970

    D. 1980

4.8 When Canada returned to international play in 1977, how did they finish at the World Championships that year?

    A. Canada won the gold medal

    B. Canada won the silver medal

    C. Canada won the bronze medal

    D. Canada finished out of medal contention

4.9 After their historic return to world play in 1977, when did Canada next win gold at the World Championships?

    A. Five years later, in 1982

    B. Nine years later, in 1986

C. Thirteen years later, in 1990

D. Seventeen years later, in 1994

4.10 How many years after Czechoslovakia split into the Czech Republic and Slovakia in 1993, did the two new countries play as opponents for the gold medal at the World Championships?

A. Four years

B. Seven years

C. 10 years

D. It has never happened

4.11 Which former NHLer played a major role in leading Slovakia from the C Pool to the A Pool of the World Championships between 1994 and 1996?

A. Peter Stastny of the Quebec Nordiques

B. Richard Zednik of the Washington Capitals

C. Peter Bondra of the Washington Capitals

D. Josef Stumpel of the Boston Bruins

4.12 At the 2002 World Championships, which former NHLer scored the historic gold-medal-winning goal for Slovakia?

A. Miroslav Satan of the Buffalo Sabres

B. Peter Bondra of the Washington Capitals

C. Josef Stumpel of the Boston Bruins

D. Ziggy Palffy of the Los Angeles Kings

4.13 In what is likely the biggest single-game comeback in World Championship history, how many consecutive goals did Sweden score to beat archrival Finland in their famous 2003 quarter-final matchup?

A. Three goals

B. Four goals

C. Five goals

D. Six goals

4.14 Canada won the 2003 World Championships after what happened during the gold-medal game against Sweden?

    A. A shootout

    B. A video review during overtime

    C. A bench-clearing brawl

    D. An electrical failure causing a loss of arena light

4.15 Between 1963 and 1986 the Soviet Union won 18 World Championships. Which sole country beat them during that 23-year span?

    A. Czechoslovakia

    B. Sweden

    C. USA

    D. Canada

4.16 In what decade were the World Junior Championships first held?

    A. The 1950s

    B. The 1960s

    C. The 1970s

    D. The 1980s

4.17 What is the record for most shootout goals by one player in one game at the World Junior Championships?

    A. Two shootout goals

    B. Three shootout goals

    C. Four shootout goals

    D. No one has ever scored more than one shootout goal in a game

4.18 A player from which country owns the IIHF record for most points at the World Championships?

    A. Czechoslovakia

    B. Canada

    C. Sweden

    D. The Soviet Union

4.19 What inspired Czechoslovakia to beat the highly favoured Soviet Union in both their games at the 1969 World Championships?

    A. A political event between their two nations

    B. A rule change that disqualified their best player

C. An unprovoked late hit that sidelined their top forward

D. A change in goaltenders

4.20 **What is the most consecutive gold medals won at the World Championships by a nation?**

A. Three straight gold medals

B. Five straight gold medals

C. Seven straight gold medals

✓ D. Nine straight gold medals

4.21 **Which team finally stopped the Soviet's record gold-medal winning streak at the 1972 World Championships?**

A. Sweden

✗ B. Czechoslovakia

C. Canada

D. Finland

4.22 **Which coach has won the most World Championships for Canada?**

A. Tom Renney

B. George Kingston

✗ C. Andy Murray

D. Dave King

4.23 **What is the IIHF player record for most World Championship titles?**

A. Six gold medals

B. Eight gold medals

✗ C. 10 gold medals

D. 12 gold medals

• • • • •ANSWERS• • • • •

Champions of the World

4.1 **D. 2008**

How is it possible that Canada, the country that invented hockey and taught the world its rules, didn't come to host the IIHF's World Championships until 2008? Taking into account that international hockey first organized itself as the Ligue Internationale de Hockey sur Glace in 1908, Canada waited 100 years to land one of hockey's most prestigious events. In the early years the Worlds were Eurocentric championships but the main stumbling block was the IIHF's refusal to permit professional players on national teams. The acrimony lasted decades and even forced Canada to abandon world competition in protest. Once the amateur-only policy was lifted, Canada returned with a greater commitment to win but it wasn't until 2003 that they applied to host the World Championships. The following year, Canada was declared host nation of the 72nd World Championships to be played in 2008, the IIHF's centennial celebration year. At those championships, the big question was whether Canada could win the gold medal and solve the home-ice curse that had plagued teams since 1986 when the Soviets won the title in Moscow. In 2008 the Canadians did reach the championship match and led Russia 4–2 going into the third period. Then, they stopped playing to protect the lead and gave up two goals in a 4–4 game. In overtime, with Rick Nash off for a delay of game penalty, Ilya Kovalchuk scored again, rifling a shot over Cam Ward's shoulder to hand Russia its first gold medal in 15 years and keep the home-ice curse alive at the World Championships.

4.2   C. Between 110 and 130 games
Jiri Holik began with the Czechoslovak national team at 19 years old and by the time he quit hockey in 1985 he had set the IIHF record by playing in 123 games in 14 World Championships. During the 1960s and 1970s, Holik was considered one of the best players on the international scene. A magnificent skater, he excelled both on offense and defense and was able to read the entire rink to control the play. He worked left wing on a line with Jan Klapac and his brother Jaroslav Holik for many years and was so reliable that he became a team fixture few felt the Czechs could do without. In the 1970s, the Detroit Red Wings tried wooing him, but he did not want to defect. In all, he scored 59 goals and 111 points on his way to three World Championships in 1972, 1976 and 1977 and four Olympic medals between 1964 and 1976. The next best numbers in games played belong to Finland's Lasse Oksanen and Vladislav Tretiak of the Soviet Union, each with 117.

Canadian captain George McAvoy shakes hands with Soviet captain Vsevolod Bobrov, as the II-HF's Bunny Ahearne presents trophies, after Canada clinched the 1955 World Championships.

4.3   B. The Trail Smoke Eaters

There was no knowing at the time, but when the Trail Smoke Eaters captured the 1961 World Championships, they became the last amateur team to win the title for Canada. Nor could anyone have envisioned when they received their gold medals that it would take Canada several decades to claim its next championship, this time with professionals in the lineup. Who were the famous world-conquering 1961 Smokies? They played in Trail, B.C., a small mining town that had a long history in hockey because the community attracted large numbers of single men to its industry. When the 1960 Allan Cup winners, the Chatham Maroons, declined to attend the 1961 Worlds in Geneva, Switzerland, their opponents in the finals, the Smoke Eaters, were invited instead. With player-coach Bobby Kromm, fleet forward Addy Tambellini and goalie Seth Martin, who gave up only 11 goals in seven games, the team played to a near-perfect 6–0–1 record and entered the final match needing to defeat the defending-champion Soviet Union by a margin of three goals to win the gold medal. Midway through the third period, with Trail leading 4–0, the Soviets scored a dramatic goal. Trail could not allow another Soviet marker since Canada had to have that three-goal spread. Then, at 17:50, in a moment that nearly rivals Paul Henderson's historic winner in 1972's Summit Series, right winger Norm Lenardon stole the puck from defenseman Nikolai Sologubov and fired it into the net. Lenardon went down on one knee and made the sign of the cross as he was mobbed by teammates, including Martin who skated the length of the ice to pile on in celebration. The four-goal cushion in their 5–1 victory guaranteed Canada the world crown once more. The Smoke Eaters were Canada's last amateur champions, made up of men working full time at the town's Cominco smelters, duelling with the all-but-professional players from Eastern Europe. Almost every member of the legendary Trail team was a hometown boy, with a few exceptions such as captain Cal Hockley, who came from nearby Fernie, B.C.

4.4   C. 1990

It wasn't until 1990 that women had their own IIHF-sanctioned championship tournament. They had been playing the game in ankle-length skirts and bloomers when men started competitive leagues during the 1890s, yet the first real attempt at a world competition would come a century later in 1987 in Toronto. University hockey and national championships aside, this event proved to be the turning point for women's hockey, inspiring other major tournaments in Europe and Asia, including the first formal Women's World Championships in 1990. Eight teams participated in the round robin and medal rounds. In the championship game, Canada beat USA 5–2 for the first-ever gold medal awarded by the IIHF in women's hockey.

4.5   A. Team members were jailed as state traitors

There was no shortage of intrigue during the darkest days of communist rule in the Soviet Union and its satellite Eastern bloc countries. Stories abound of secret police, defections, state kidnappings and spy networks that kept citizens behind what Winston

Churchill called an "iron curtain" of forced internment. Under such a totalitarian regime, no one could travel to the West, with exceptions given mainly to artists and athletes. Hockey, because of its popularity, became a propaganda tool in communicating the superiority of the Soviet way of life; and winning was seen as a victory for communism. But the price came high, as conspiracy theories dogged most athletes with travel papers. And even though they were world champions, the Czechoslovak national team was not above suspicion, as they found out in March 1950, just before boarding a plane, en route to defending their title at the championships in London, England. In one dramatic moment, players were handcuffed by Czechoslovak national security police and thrown in jail, accused of attempting to defect and charged with treason. Seven months later they appeared in court and all 12 players were found guilty of being traitors. Their sentences ranged from eight months to 15 years. Whatever proof came to light was suspect, as none of the accused ever seriously contemplated defecting.

4.6 B. Finland

The Anaheim Ducks are not the only hockey team to take inspiration from the animated characters of the Walt Disney Company. At the same time that the Mighty Ducks entered the NHL in the early 1990s, in Europe, Finland's coach Curt Lindstrom saw the potential in a kid line with Saku Koivu, Ville Peltonen and Jere Lehtinen for the 1994 Lillehammer Olympics. Soon, the threesome was dubbed the "Donald Duck Line" and nicknamed individually as Tupu, Hupu and Lupu—Finnish for Uncle Donald's nephew triplets, Huey, Dewey and Louie. The trio clicked immediately. Finland captured Olympic bronze and, a few months later, the silver at the 1994 World Championships. While the medals certainly validated Finland's development program, the Nordic nation was long overdue for a title after many frustrating seasons of near-triumphs through almost two decades in the world arena. Then, the following year, Tupu, Hupu and Lupu were united again at the 1995 Worlds in Stockholm, where the Finns earned a berth in the final against Sweden and another chance at gold. This time they made no mistakes with a 4–1 win against the Swedes as Peltonen scored a hat trick and assisted on the fourth goal. Tupu, Hupu and Lupu were all named to the tournament's All-Star Team and Tupu (Koivu) was honoured as top forward of the event. It remains Finland's only gold medal to date.

4.7   C. 1970

After capturing gold at the 1961 World Championships, but precious little else during the 1960s, Canada finally withdrew from competition in 1970, leaving in protest over the thorny issue of amateur-only participation at IIHF events. Canada realized that after dominating world hockey since the 1920s, their amateurs could no longer compete effectively against the top European national teams, especially the Soviets, who were amateur in name only, considering they trained and played together 11 months of the year. What Canadian hockey authorities wanted was an "open" competition and they were temporarily successful in their bid when the IIHF permitted a few mediocre professionals to play at the annual Izvestija Cup in December 1969. The Canadians finished second with five pros in the lineup, but the point was made in a surprise 2–2 tie against the Soviets. That game likely caused some concern for the amateur establishment because the following year the IIHF backtracked on the ruling to allow professionals, with Olympic president Avery Brundage weighing in heavily against amateurs and professionals playing together. Canada responded forcefully and refused to host the 1970 World Championships slated for Montreal and Winnipeg. More significantly, they pulled out of international competition altogether, snubbing the World Championships and the Olympics until 1977, when modern eligibility rules were adopted that eliminated any categorization of players, amateur or pro.

4.8   D. Canada finished out of medal contention

It was neither pretty nor glorious when Canada took to international ice again in 1977 after seven years of isolation. However, just being there, playing against the world's best teams, was in itself a triumph. Altogether, the Canadians had missed seven World Championships and two Olympics in their showdown with the IIHF. But now they were back, icing a roster of high-quality NHL veterans, including Phil and Tony Espositio, Rod Gilbert, Pierre Larouche and Ron Ellis. Unfortunately, Canada's squad came to Europe ill-prepared with no real game plan or knowledge of how hockey had progressed since their departure in 1970. In fact, they still played the old-time hockey using size and strength, instead of the kind of speed and skill displayed by the elite European clubs. While the team played well against some opponents, they got clocked by scores of 11–1 and 8–1 in their two games versus the Soviet Union. Worse, their lack of success led to frustration and, as a result, many games were marred with scenes of ugly violence—the worst offender was Wilf Paiement, who amassed 32 penalty minutes in 10 games. For the first time, Canada had sent a lineup of NHL players to the Worlds and, by some accounts, it proved a disaster. They were scorned in Europe for many years to come after the debacle of 1977. But the big hit to their sporting reputation came from the immediate disappointment and ridicule back home, after their fourth-place finish behind Czechoslovakia, Sweden and the Soviets.

4.9   **D. Seventeen years later, in 1994**

While Canada's return to international hockey in 1977 signalled a new accord with the IIHF, their ruling to allow NHLers in world competition did little to produce immediate dividends in gold medals for the Canadians. In the next 14 World Championships, the country that was virtually unbeatable for 30 years until the mid-1950s could now do no better than a handful of silvers and bronzes. Finally, in 1994, Canada struck gold again in Milan, Italy. With a roster of Canadian NHLers eliminated from the Stanley Cup playoffs that included Joe Sakic, Jason Arnott, Brendan Shanahan and Rob Blake, Canada mowed down every competitor in the round robin, then snipped the Czech Republic 3–2 and shutout Sweden 6–0 in the playoff rounds to reach the highly dramatic finals against Finland. For Finn sniper Jari Kurri, it was his lowest point in his international career. "We were leading 1–0 with some minutes left and killing a power play when Rod Brind'Amour tripped me at centre ice," said Kurri in the book *World of Hockey*. "It was a clear penalty, but the ref didn't call it and Brind'Amour walked in and scored the tying goal." Ten minutes of overtime decided nothing and the shootout was on with each team scoring twice. Then, Luc Robitaille skated in on Jarmo Myllys, lost control of the puck, regained possession in time to make a masterful deke on the Finnish goalie. Canada ended a 33-year gold-medal drought that dated back to the Trail Smoke Eaters' victory in 1961.

4.10 B. Seven years

While the political and geographic breakup of Czechoslovakia was bloodless, its dissolution didn't come without tearing apart national institutions such as the Czechoslovak hockey program. The split of the former Eastern bloc country into the Czech Republic and Slovakia on January 1, 1993, saw each country ice its own team with the Czechs maintaining the position of former Czechoslovakia and the Slovaks becoming a new hockey nation in the IIHF system. As a result, tiny Slovakia started at the bottom in Pool C at the 1994 World Championships and had to play through the divisions, quickly reaching the elite Pool A two years later in 1996. Their steady development with national team players such as Ziggy Palffy, Miroslav Satan and Pavol Demitra led to the 2000 Worlds in St. Petersburg, Russia, where on May 14 the two independent nations played for the gold-medal game, just seven years after their historic separation. Although the Czech Republic defeated their former compatriots 5–3 to win the world title, the outcome was significantly less important than the moment itself, as the two elite hockey powers showed the world the might of the old Czechoslovak hockey program.

4.11 A. Peter Stastny of the Quebec Nordiques

Few players have had a more profound influence on NHL and international hockey than Peter Stastny. In fact, given his contributions to both Czechoslovakia and his true country Slovakia on the international stage and his record at the NHL level, Stastny's impact on the game is unparalleled. Born in Bratislava, Czechoslovakia, he was thrust into hockey's limelight at 19 when he starred on the Czech team and won a surprising gold medal at the 1976 World Championships. After another gold and two silvers at the Worlds, Stastny, at 24 years old, was considered among Europe's leading players. Then, in 1980, he defected to the NHL, where he notched seven 100-point seasons and finished second only to Wayne Gretzky as top point earner during the 1980s. A staunch patriot, Stastny brought his leadership and gamesmanship to the Slovak team after Slovakia gained independence from Czechoslovakia in the early

1990s. And Slovakia's needs were great, considering their placement in Pool C of the world rankings. At the 1994 Olympics, Stastny carried the Slovak flag at the opening ceremonies in Lillehammer, Norway, and led his squad to an unexpected sixth-place finish after scoring nine points in eight games. A few weeks later, without Stastny, who had a commitment to the St. Louis Blues, the Slovak team won the C Pool of the World Championships. The following year, destiny brought Stastny's career full circle in his final competition when the hero of Bratislava suited up again, this time before a hometown crowd at the B-Pool World Championships. Stastny's 16 points in six games helped Slovakia claim the tournament and move his nation up the ranks to the A Pool. It was a stunning final performance, one that came on the 20th anniversary of his debut with the Czechoslovak national club. He retired from playing but was instrumental once more as general manager of the Slovak program, guiding his team to the 1998 and 2002 Olympics and, then, at the 2002 Worlds when Slovakia made history and won the gold. In three short years, Stastny had advanced Slovakia from C to A Pool and six years later established his country as an international hockey force to challenge the top six hockey nations on the planet.

4.12   B. Peter Bondra of the Washington Capitals

When the Slovak national team beat Russia 4–3 at the 2002 World Championships in Sweden, the gold-medal victory represented validation not only for a hockey team in the international arena, but for an independent nation and its place in the world. The hero was Peter Bondra, who broke a 3–3 tie with a goal against Russia with just 100 seconds remaining in the third period of the championship match. The NHL veteran combined with Ziggy Palffy on a pretty two-on-one break, as Palffy fed a perfect pass to Bondra streaking in on the left wing. From near the faceoff dot, Bondra whipped a blast at Maxim Sokolov that sneaked past the goalie's attempted kick save, struck the inside post and ricocheted into the net. The famed goal on May 11 lit up the Slovak world as if independence from the old Soviet republic of Czechoslovakia had been declared all over again. Following the game, players kissed the Scandinavian ice in celebration, team manager Peter Stastny cried on the bench and back home millions of fans celebrated wildly throughout the country. "This means more than a Stanley

Cup to me," said Bondra. "The Cup is celebrated by one city. This belongs to an entire nation."

4.13   C. Five goals

Among international hockey's great rivalries, few compare in bitterness to that between Nordic adversaries Sweden and Finland. Their history in hockey, like their geography—the two nations share 380 miles of border—is linked by close association and a national passion for the game. And, unfortunately for Finland, the Swedes typically dominate their on-ice match-ups. Perhaps the Finns most excruciating loss came on home turf at Hartwall Areena in Helsinki during quarter-final action of the 2003 World Championships. Finland held an impressive 5–1 lead midway through the second period before Swedish coach Hardy Nilsson pulled goaltender Tommy Salo in favour of backup Mikael Tellqvist. The momentum suddenly shifted and Sweden charged back with five unanswered goals, silencing the Finnish crowd and leaving their squad stunned in disbelief at their collapse. P.J. Axelsson scored the game-winner on the power play at 15:06, with Saku Koivu in the penalty box for high-sticking. Interestingly, Koivu was the goat on another occasion against the Swedes when his stick broke on a third-period faceoff with a 2–2 score during the gold-medal game at the 2006 Winter Games. The incident left Koivu's club shorthanded long enough for a Nicklas Lidstrom slapshot to slip past Antero Niittymaki for the Olympic winner. Again the Finns had succumbed to pressure from Sweden, this time in finals play, to lose the gold. As of 2009, a tally of their lifetime box score against each other in Olympic and World Championship competition totaled 40 wins by the Swedes compared to 15 victories for Finland.

4.14   B. A video review during overtime

Among the top six hockey nations, few teams have provided Canadian fans with more heart-stopping finales in gold-medal showdowns than Sweden. In 1991, it was Mats Sundin's third-period goal against the Soviet Union in the championship match that denied Canada the gold medal based on goal differential. Then, at the 1994 Olympics, Peter Forsberg's heroics in a thrilling shootout again upset Canada's gold-medal chances in the

3–2 squeaker. And the 1997 Worlds provided more gold-medal drama when Sweden fell short 2–1 after scoring a last-minute gut-wrencher. But, perhaps the most nerve-racking spectacle in the annals of Sweden-Canada showdowns came in 2003 when Anson Carter swooped in from behind the net to tuck the puck under Mikael Tellqvist's pad at 13:49 in overtime. The Canadian team erupted in celebration, but clearly the 2–2 game wasn't settled. Czech referee Vladimir Sindler had no clear view of the puck before it eventually came out again. With the gold medal on the line, Sindler went upstairs to video goal judge Pavel Halas to determine whether the puck had completely crossed the line. After several anxious minutes for both sides, Halas found the correct camera angle and the puck was about 15 centimetres over the goal line. "It's the best goal of my career," Carter said. "To score in overtime period to win gold for your country, I don't think it gets bigger than that."

4.15   A. Czechoslovakia

The Czechoslovak national team first came to prominence immediately following World War II, when they became the first European squad to challenge Canada's number one ranking in international competition with titles at the 1947 (with Canada absent) and 1949 World Championships, and a silver-medal finish at the 1948 Olympics, losing the gold only by a goal differential to Canada. Then, their hockey program suffered a severe blow in 1950 when several team members were jailed on trumped-up charges of treason by the Stalinist Czechoslovak government. The Czechs took years to rebuild their system but rebounded with some of the most creative playmakers on European ice, including forwards Vladimir Martinec, Jiri Holik and Ivan Hlinka, Frantisek Pospisil on defense and Vladimir Dzurilla between the pipes. Between 1963 and 1986, when the Soviets' Big Red Machine amassed 18 World titles, Czechoslovakia finished second 10 times and won four crowns in 1972, 1976, 1977 and 1985, becoming the only gold medalists, other than the Soviets, of that era.

4.16   C. The 1970s

More popular in Canada than anywhere else in the world, the World Juniors has earned a special place in the hearts of millions

Team Canada's Patrice Bergeron, Sidney Crosby and Corey Perry celebrate after defeating Russia 6–1 to win the 2005 World Junior Championships in Grand Forks, North Dakota.

of hockey fans who look forward each Christmas and New Years to watching the world's next superstars compete for the title of under-20 hockey champions. The event evolved from Canada's protests over its inability to use professionals at major events during the 1960s. As a result, in 1970, Canada withdrew its national teams from world play, leaving no place on the calendar for young players and true amateurs to compete internationally. To fill the void, an invitational tournament was initiated in 1974 and two years later the World Juniors received full IIHF status. Like the players it showcases, the event went through its own growing pains. But it never failed to deliver the world's best teenagers on ice, including Wayne Gretzky, Dominik Hasek and Alexander Ovechkin, each of whom appeared in at least one tournament. Today, the World Juniors has become a hockey tradition for fans everywhere, with a popularity that has produced strong rivalries between competing nations. More significantly, it is an important proving ground for player performance, used by pro scouts to measure the quality of play of the next generation of stars.

4.17   B. Three shootout goals

In one of the most thrilling sudden-death shootouts in World Junior history, Canada's Jonathan Toews scored a record three times as coach Craig Hartsburg kept putting the 18-year-old out in a seven-round shootout during the 2007 semi-final matchup against rival USA. The game was tied 1–1 through 60 minutes of regulation time on goals by Taylor Chorney for the Americans and Luc Bourdon of Canada, and then another 10-minute overtime with Canadian netminder Carey Price providing the heroics as the Americans had a 12–2 shots advantage in the four-on-four play. That set the stage for the dramatic shootout between Price and USA goalie Jeffrey Frazee. In the first round of three shooters per team, each side scored twice, including one high over Frazee's glove by Toews. The game then went into sudden-death shootouts—one shot per team—with each coach choosing any player from his bench to go one-on-one. Frazee and Price stopped the next set of shooters, but gave up successive goals in the two following rounds, as Toews earned another goal through the five-hole to keep Canada in contention. In the next shootout series, Hartsburg called on Toews a third time and the 18-year old scored his third goal. "I guess I was running out of ways to score so I gave him a little head fake," said Toews. "He was further out of the net and I was able to beat him on the blocker side." Then, Price stopped Peter Mueller (who had already scored twice in the shootout) on USA's next attempt and Canada was off to the championship match, which they won against Russia.

4.18   D. The Soviet Union

He has been called the best sniper in the history of Soviet hockey and that may be still understating the excellence of Boris Mikhailov. In 500 Soviet-league games for CSKA Moscow he racked up an incredible 428 goals as one of the most fearsome weapons in the dominant Soviet arsenal of the 1970s. But it was his mental game that set him apart. Although he was never an elegant skater, nor as inventive as linemate Valeri Kharlamov, Mikhailov's genius lay in "his ruthlessness, his hunger to score and his desire for victory, regardless of the finer details of the play," observed the authors of *Kings of the Ice*. Once he got the puck, he usually scored, especially in deep, crashing the net where he was most dangerous. One third of the celebrated "Army Line" of Mikhailov, Kharlamov and Vladimir Petrov, Mikhailov scored an IIHF all-time record 169 points in World Championship action.

Most IIHF World Championship Points*

PLAYER	COUNTRY	POINTS
Boris Mikhailov	Soviet Union	169
Valeri Kharlamov	Soviet Union	159
Alexander Maltsev	Soviet Union	159
Vladimir Petrov	Soviet Union	154
Sven Tumba	Sweden	127

*Current to 2009

4.19 A. A political event between their two nations

The 1969 World Championships will be remembered less for who won the six-team tournament than for the matchup between the Soviet and Czech national teams. Just seven months earlier, Soviet forces crushed Czechoslovakia when Warsaw Pact tanks rumbled through the streets of Prague to halt countrywide reforms made by the liberal Czechoslovak government. There was no military resistance during the occupation, but the Czechs surrendered nothing in their all-out war on the ice. At the Worlds in Sweden, they made sure to beat the Soviet team, 2–0 and 4–3, in their two clashes often described as the most emotionally charged games in international hockey history. "We said to ourselves, even if we have to die on the ice, we have to beat them," captain Jozef Golonka said later. Alas, the Czechs didn't have enough fight left in them to defeat Sweden and settled for a bronze medal based on goal differential, while the Soviets deservedly took home their seventh consecutive championship.

4.20 D. Nine straight gold medals

After their stunning debut at the 1954 World Championships, the Soviets didn't take long to establish themselves as one of hockey's top nations. Their gold-medal victory against Canada was the first historic faceoff between the two hockey superpowers and it sent a clear warning to Canadian hockey authorities that a new force was ready to challenge the 30-year dominance of their amateurs on the world circuit. Canada exacted revenge in 1955 by winning back top honours but the Soviets took Olympic gold at Cortina, Italy, in 1956. After that, Canada managed few golds while the Soviet Union stockpiled seven Olympic and 19 World Championship gold medals until its demise with the collapse of communism in 1991. Soviet reign was absolute during a decade-long dynasty run from 1963 to 1971 when they were near invincible through nine consecutive World crowns (which included two Olympics). They simply monopolized the game, amassing an astounding record of 64 wins versus only six losses and two ties in 72 games. The Soviets routinely outscored their opponents by a goal ratio of five or six to one for a scoring aggregate of 520 goals for and only 116 against. No country, not even Canada, has ever ruled so completely as the Soviets at their height of power.

4.21 B. Czechoslovakia

As the undisputed champions of world hockey with nine straight World Championships and a trio of Olympic victories since 1963, the Soviets were certain favourites to capture an unprecedented 10th world title at the 1972 Worlds in Czechoslovakia. But their march was dramatically and ironically stopped in the host city, Prague, the site of the Prague Spring rebellion, where four years earlier 200,000 Warsaw Pact troops entered and occupied the country. Now, with the great Vladimir Dzurilla in goal and Jaroslav Holik, Vaclav Nedomansky and Ivan Hlinka upfront, battling the Soviet Union's Vladislav Tretiak, Valeri Kharlamov, Alexander Yakushev and Boris Mikhailov, came some sweet payback for the Czechs as they upset their political adversaries in a 3–2 victory that eventually earned Czechoslovakia the gold and stopped the Soviet streak of nine titles. This triumph in Prague, before home fans hungry for revenge against the Soviet empire, sent the entire Czech nation into pandemonium. It remains one of the greatest victories ever in hockey history, European or otherwise.

4.22 C. Andy Murray

"If they want me to drive the bus or carry the sticks, I'm a proud Canadian and I'll always be there if they ask me," responded Andy Murray, about his interests in coaching Canada's Olympic team in 2010. Murray had just turned in a gold-medal performance with a team that had only a few star players but won all nine games at the 2007 World Championships. His reputation for taking franchises to the next level by inspiring players and stressing teamwork earned him a eye-popping 23–2–2 record for his third gold, after championships in 1997 and 2003, each with three completely different rosters. No Canadian coach has ever won more than one championship, which says as much as Murray's coaching abilities as his sense of patriotism. And judging by his repeated success internationally, his country comes first when it wants his European hockey smarts and analytical approach to the game. Still, because the Worlds are held during the NHL postseason, he'd rather see the next Team Canada lineup with another coach. "The only job I'm worried about now is trying to get the St. Louis Blues in the playoffs," said Murray in 2007.

4.23 C. 10 gold medals

All the top rankings in this category are owned by Soviet players who amassed multiple medals during their country's rise to international glory at the World Championships, where their extraordinary run of titles continued almost uninterrupted between 1963 and 1986. During that span, goalie Vladislav Tretiak and Alexander Ragulin struck gold an IIHF record ten times. Between the Worlds and Olympics, Tretiak is the most successful player in international hockey history. Including his 10 golds, two silvers and one bronze at the Worlds, the Russian netminder also won three Olympic golds and one silver; and one Canada Cup in 1981.

Most IIHF World Championship medals

PLAYER	COUNTRY	SEASONS	MEDAL COUNT
Vladislav Tretiak	Soviet Union	1970–1983	G-10 S-2 B-1
Alexander Ragulin	Soviet Union	1961–1973	G*-10 S-1 B-1

*includes medals in 1964 and 1968 Olympic games
which also counted as World Championships

••• GAME 4 •••

The Granites, Mercurys and Smoke Eaters

CANADA HAS A RICH legacy of international representation by senior amateur teams from across the country. Perhaps the most familiar name is the Smoke Eaters, the club from Trail B.C. that holds the distinction of being Canada's last amateur winners of the World Championships. Their team nickname came after one memorable game in 1928 when fans littered the ice with debris. Trail's player-coach Carroll Kendall picked up one item, a still-smoking pipe, and played the rest of his shift puffing away on it. An editorial cartoon the next day dubbed the Trail team "a bunch of smoke-eaters" and the name stuck. It survives still today. In this game, match the team and year at the Worlds to their colourful nicknames.

Solutions are on page 139.

1. 1924 – Toronto _____   A. Mercurys

2. 1934 – Saskatoon _____   B. Dynamiters

3. 1935 – Winnipeg _____   C. Quakers

4. 1936 – Port Arthur _____   D. Dunlops

5. 1937 – Kimberley _____   E. Flyers

6. 1938 – Sudbury _____   F. Granites

7. 1948 – RCAF _____   G. Dutchmen

8. 1950 – Edmonton _____   H. Bearcats

9. 1954 – Whitby _____   I. Wolves

10. 1956 – Kitchener-Waterloo ___   J. Monarchs

5

THE MARCH WEST

HOW FAR HAS THE game progressed since NHLers first battled the stoic Soviet players of the 1970s? Today, the most entertaining player in the NHL is a glass-crashing, stick-too-hot-to-handle, Don Cherry–baiting Russian named Alexander Ovechkin, who drives Washington Capitals fans into a frenzy with his wild goal-scoring celebrations. The image must have former hockey czar Viktor Tikhonov downing double shots of vodka in despair. In this chapter, we imbibe in a little celebrating of our own and check out how Russian and European players have contributed to the NHL talent pool with this series of league firsts.

Answers are on page 98

5.1 Who was the first European-trained goalie to start an NHL game?
A. Hardy Astrom of Sweden
B. Jiri Crha of Czechoslovakia
C. Markus Mattsson of Finland
D. Pelle Lindbergh of Sweden

5.2 Although Czech goalie Jiri Crha defected to the NHL before any other European, who was the first high-profile player to escape the Iron Curtain and play in the NHL?
A. Peter Stastny
B. Jari Kurri
C. Petr Svoboda
D. Viacheslav Fetisov

5.3 Who was the first European to be selected first overall in the NHL Entry Draft?
A. Bjorn Johansson of Sweden
B. Petr Svoboda of Czechoslovakia
C. Mats Sundin of Sweden
D. Teemu Selanne of Finland

5.4 Who was the first Soviet player to defect and play in the NHL?

A. Sergei Fedorov

B. Alexander Mogilny

C. Igor Larionov

D. Pavel Bure

5.5 Which team hired the first European-trained head coach?

A. The Pittsburgh Penguins

B. The Detroit Red Wings

C. The Washington Capitals

D. The Chicago Blackhawks

5.6 What league first did Swedish forward Ulf Sterner achieve in the NHL?

A. He was the first European-trained NHLer

B. He was the first European-trained player in an NHL fight

C. He was the first European-trained draft pick in NHL history

D. He was the first European-trained NHL trophy winner

5.7 Who was the first Soviet player to be drafted by an NHL team?

A. Viacheslav Fetisov, by the Montreal Canadiens

B. Viktor Khatulev, by the Philadelphia Flyers

C. Sergei Makarov, by the Calgary Flames

D. Vladislav Tretiak, by the Montreal Canadiens

5.8 Which team finally brought Soviet great Vladislav Tretiak to the NHL?

A. The Montreal Canadiens

B. The Chicago Blackhawks

C. The Winnipeg Jets

D. The New York Rangers

5.9 Who was the first Soviet-trained player to score an NHL goal?

A. Viktor Nechayev of the Los Angeles Kings

B. Viacheslav Fetisov of the New Jersey Devils

C. Sergei Priakhin of the Calgary Flames

D. Igor Larionov of the Vancouver Canucks

5.10 Who was the first European-trained player to captain an NHL team?

A. Stan Mikita of the Chicago Blackhawks

B. Mats Sundin of the Toronto Maple Leafs

C. Peter Stastny of the Quebec Nordiques

D. Lars-Erik Sjoberg of the Winnipeg Jets

5.11 Who was the first European-trained goalie to win the Vezina Trophy?

A. Dominik Hasek of Czechoslovakia

B. Pelle Lindbergh of Sweden

C. Tommy Salo of Sweden

D. Roman Turek of Czechoslovakia

5.12 In what season did Europeans first sweep first, second and third place in the NHL scoring race?

A. 1993–94

B. 1995–96

C. 1997–98

D. 1998–99

5.13 The first European-trained player to score 50 goals in a season came from which country?

A. Czechoslovakia

B. Finland

C. Sweden

D. The Soviet Union

5.14 Which NHL team was first to retire a sweater number worn by a European-trained player?

A. The Winnipeg Jets

B. The Edmonton Oilers

C. The New York Islanders

D. The Toronto Maple Leafs

5.15 Who was the first European-trained starting goalie to lead his team to the Stanley Cup?

A. Nikolai Khabibulin of Russia

B. Dominik Hasek of Czechoslovakia

C. David Aebischer of Switzerland

D. Ilya Bryzgalov of the Russia

5.16 Which NHL team was the first to win the Stanley Cup with a European-trained player on its roster?

A. The Philadelphia Flyers

B. The Montreal Canadiens

C. The New York Islanders

D. The Edmonton Oilers

5.17 Name the only team to win the Stanley Cup since 1980 without a European-trained player on its roster?

A. The Montreal Canadiens in 1993

B. The Colorado Avalanche in 2001

C. The New Jersey Devils in 2003

D. The Anaheim Ducks in 2007

5.18 The Detroit Red Wings' five-man Russian unit played a key role in the team's march to the 1997 Stanley Cup. In how many of Detroit's 16 playoff wins that year did one of its five players score a point?

A. Nine wins

B. 11 wins

C. 13 wins

D. 15 wins

5.19 Who was the first Russian-trained scorer in a Stanley Cup final?

A. Igor Kravchuk of the Chicago Blackhawks

B. Alexei Kovalev of the New York Rangers

C. Alexei Zhitnik of the Los Angeles Kings

D. Pavel Bure of the Vancouver Canucks

5.20 Which team iced the first European-trained player to appear in the Stanley Cup finals?

A. The Toronto Maple Leafs

B. The Calgary Flames

C. The New York Rangers

D. The Boston Bruins

5.21 Who was the first European-trained player to score a goal in the Stanley Cup finals?
  A. Anders Hedberg of the New York Rangers in 1979
  B. Ulf Nilsson of the New York Rangers in 1979
  C. Stefan Persson of the New York Islanders in 1980
  D. Kent-Lars Andersson of the Minnesota North Stars in 1981

5.22 Who was the first European-trained NHLer inducted into the Hockey Hall of Fame?
  A. Peter Stastny of Slovakia
  B. Vladislav Tretiak of Russia
  C. Borje Salming of Sweden
  D. Mats Naslund of Sweden

• • • • ANSWERS • • • •

The March West

5.1 **A. Hardy Astrom of Sweden**

On February 25, 1978, New York Rangers coach Jean-Guy Talbot played a desperate hunch and gave Swedish rookie Hardy Astrom the starting assignment in a game against the Montreal Canadiens on Forum ice. Few goalies have ever experienced a more intimidating NHL debut. The dynasty Canadiens, in the midst of a four Stanley Cup run, were riding an NHL record 28-game unbeaten streak. Meanwhile, the Rangers had not won a game at the Forum in six seasons. For Astrom, the occasion was doubly significant: it was his first NHL match and the first start by a European netminder. But, despite the odds, he played brilliantly, sparking the Rangers to a 6–3 victory. It was a rare highlight in an otherwise undistinguished career for Astrom, as he saw action in only three more games for the Rangers, and was later traded to the woeful Colorado Rockies. There, he played two miserable years for coach Don Cherry, who took delight in heaping abuse on the European, calling Astrom "my Swedish sieve."

5.2 A. Peter Stastny

When Peter Stastny famously joined the Quebec Nordiques in 1980, he was among Europe's premier players. Stastny had starred for five years with Slovan in the Czech Elite League and in 1979–80 he was named Czechoslovak Player of the Year after notching 26 goals and 52 points in only 41 games. But all that changed with one phone call during the 1980 European Cup in Innsbruck, Austria. Stastny contacted the Quebec Nordiques' general manager Marcel Aubut in the hopes of playing with the fledging Nordiques in the NHL and in an effort escape to communist-controlled Czechoslovakia. Stastny had been warned that his public statements criticizing the communist regime in Czechoslovakia would end his hockey career. "This is when I realized... there was no future for me [in Czechoslovakia], as a player or a person," said Stastny. His dramatic defection (he was accompanied by his pregnant wife Darina and his brother Anton, who also played with Slovan) had all the intrigue of a Cold War spy novel. Aubut immediately flew to Innsbruck to negotiate with the brothers. In covert meetings during the tournament, he agreed to sign the pair and help them escape after the final game on August 24. Under darkness, with everything to lose if they got caught, the trio fled Innsbruck, made it through airport customs and boarded a plane booked by Aubut for Canada. Stastny had given up his family, his homeland and everything known to him, with little assurance about what the future held. While Czechs had defected before (Vaclav Nedomansky and Richard Farda to the rival WHA in 1974; and Jiri Crha to the NHL in 1979), the Stastnys' escape stunned the hockey world and made headlines around the globe. For the underachieving Nordiques, it brought instant respectability as the brothers finished first and third in team scoring on this franchise that was playoff-bound just one year after their merger as a WHA team into the NHL. Internationally, the Stastny defections were trailblazing, forcing Eastern bloc nations to rethink their hardline policies for veteran stars and inspiring all players to dream of an NHL career.

5.3 C. Mats Sundin of Sweden

The slow process of globalizing the NHL began with the seminal signings of free agents Borje Salming and Inge Hammarstrom by the Toronto Maple Leafs in 1973. But it wasn't until 1989 that the league awarded its top draft to a non–North American. During that time, NHL general managers gambled on a flood of European talent, some turning into flops, such as Bjorn Johansson, the first European taken in the first round (fifth overall in 1976), others becoming important team additions, players such as Kent Nilsson (64th in 1976), Jari Kurri (69th in 1980), Ulf Samuelsson (67th in 1982), Igor Larionov (214th in 1985), Teppo Numminen (29th in 1986) and Teemu Selanne (10th in 1988). As talented as these players were, Mats Sundin was the first European chosen first overall in the draft. At just 19 years old, while still a junior with Djurgarden, he was signed by the cellar-dwelling Quebec Nordiques. Although he has had a brilliant NHL career, playing annually at the NHL All-Star Game, it is his international work representing Tre Kronor that has brought Sundin his most impressive credentials, with six medals at the World Championships, including three golds and an Olympic gold medal in 2006.

5.4 B. Alexander Mogilny

The first Soviet hockey star to defect to the NHL was Alexander Mogilny, who bolted the USSR at the 1989 World Championships in Sweden. Just a year earlier, Mogilny, then 20 years old, was the toast of European hockey, as the youngest Soviet player ever to win an Olympic gold medal—which he did at the Calgary Games in 1988. But that all changed with his defection and subsequent rendezvous in an undercover operation with representatives of the Buffalo Sabres in Stockholm in May 1989. "Even the KGB didn't know about it," said Viacheslav Fetisov, then captain of the Soviet championship team. "I was trying to find a legal way to open things up [to play in the NHL] and all of a sudden somebody finds a different way," said Fetisov, who was finally released to play in the NHL several months after Mogilny defected. In the Soviet Union, Mogilny, a conscripted officer in the army, was tried in absentia and found guilty of desertion. "I couldn't see myself growing as a person and as a hockey player in Russia at that time. I didn't see any different way to do it," said Mogilny. As a tribute to his defection year he chose to sweater number 89. By fluke or by fate, Buffalo drafted Mogilny in 1988, 89th overall.

5.5 D. The Chicago Blackhawks

After signing a three-year contract in February 2000 as assistant coach with Pittsburgh, Czech native Ivan Hlinka looked to be the replacement for the Penguins' Herb Brooks and the first European-born-and-bred head coach in the NHL. But Chicago director of hockey operations Mike Smith, being no stranger to international hockey, hired Finnish native Alpo Suhonen in April 2000, just prior to Hlinka's appointment with Pittsburgh in June of that year. Each had an extensive coaching resume with Suhonen behind the bench for more than 1,500 games in Europe and 300 as an assistant coach in the NHL, and Hlinka, who had built his country's ice hockey program into one of the world's best and coached the gold-medal-winning 1998 Czech Olympic team. The hiring of two European-trained coaches after 82 years of NHL play (Russian-born Johnny Gottselig coached Chicago in the mid-1940s but was raised in Winnipeg) broke "new ground," as longtime coach Dave King said, but their tenures were brief. Suhonen coached 82 games in 2000–01 and Hlinka just 86 between the 2000-01 and 2001-02 seasons.

5.6 A. He was the first European-trained NHLer

Borje Salming may be the most recognizable name among early European pioneers in the NHL, but eight years before Salming made hockey headlines with the Toronto Maple Leafs in 1973, there was Ulf Sterner. His talent as a complete skill player was quickly recognized in homeland Sweden, where he became the youngest player on the national team at 17 years old. The following year he made his world debut at the 1960 Olympics and during the next four years he became an international star, leading Tre Kronor to the podium multiple times, including in 1962 when he scored twice in Sweden's historic 5–3 gold-medal victory against heavily favoured Canada at the World Championships in Colorado Springs, Colorado. Then, in 1963, the New York Rangers came calling, but Sterner declined, worried about maintaining his amateur status for the upcoming Olympics. The Rangers finally signed him for 1964–65 and after some adjustments to North American play in the minors he made his debut on January 27, 1965, to become the first European-trained player in the NHL. But Sterner never registered a point and only stayed four games, unhappy with his coach's demands to "play tougher and shoot on goal more often," as Sterner later said. To his point, the physical demands of professional hockey ran contrary to European training, which forbade bodychecking in the offensive zone. He returned home and continued his international career for another decade. Today, Ulf Sterner is recognized as among the best players Sweden has ever produced.

5.7 B. Viktor Khatulev, by the Philadelphia Flyers

While Soviet restrictions on player availability made it literally impossible for NHL teams to sign Russian talent before perestroika in 1989, several North American clubs still gambled late draft picks on a select few players during the 1970s and 1980s. Despite the long shot of actually bagging a Russian, the first team to risk a selection was the Philadelphia Flyers with their 160th pick of Dynamo Riga centre Viktor Khatulev in 1975. Predictably, Khatulev never played for the Flyers, but his selection was fitting for the NHL's most penalized team. Khatulev was a certified goon, who was banned for one year and, later, for life for on-ice violence in the Soviet leagues. Three years after his pick, in 1978, Montreal chose 20-year old defenseman Viacheslav Fetisov 201st overall. It proved to be another wasted pick, although Fetisov re-entered the NHL Draft in 1983 with New Jersey, played several seasons for the Devils during the 1990s and twice won the Stanley Cup as a Detroit Red Wing in 1997 and 1998. As for Sergei Makarov, drafted by Calgary in 1983—he didn't join the Flames until 1989. However, among all the early Russian draftees, none had more potential to make a big-league impact than Montreal's choice of world-class goalie Vladislav Tretiak in 1983. Regrettably, his move to the NHL was also blocked by the Soviet government and Tretiak decided to retire in 1984. He was just 32 years old.

5.8 B. The Chicago Blackhawks

Although it was the Montreal Canadiens' Serge Savard who secured Vladislav Tretiak's playing rights by drafting him 138th in the 1983 Entry Draft, his eventual passport into the NHL would be as a goaltending consultant with Chicago in 1990. Tretiak had retired prematurely in 1984—with likely several more able-bodied years of play in him—after the Soviet Red Army team would not release him. When he finally came to North America, his first assignment was tutoring the Blackhawks' rookie netminder, Ed Belfour (and his backup Dominik Hasek). Tretiak clearly had an impact. In 1990–91, Belfour walked away with a trio of trophies: the Vezina as top goalie, the Jennings for allowing the fewest goals and the Calder as outstanding rookie. Later, Belfour wore No. 20 on his sweater to honour Tretiak, his most influential goalie coach. The Soviet goaltender never played in the NHL but his famous jersey number endured on the back of his star pupil.

5.9   A. Viktor Nechayev of the Los Angeles Kings

The modest career of Viktor Nechayev has few high points. An average centre playing for SKA Leningrad who skated well and had a great shot, Nechayev found his way to North America by marrying an American graduate student studying abroad in Leningrad. That gave him American residency; and on an impulse, he was drafted 132nd overall in 1982 by Los Angeles, where he became a media darling of sorts. However, the Kings were anything but impressed and Nechayev survived only three games (as a replacement to a trio of injured centres). He scored just one NHL goal on October 17, 1982, against the New York Rangers at Madison Square Garden, but it was enough to make him the league's very first Soviet goal scorer. Despite his blip of glory, Nechayev cannot claim the status of Sergei Priakhin, who, seven years later in 1989, became the first Soviet player to officially transfer to the NHL with the approval of the Soviet Ice Hockey Federation. Priakhin played with Krylya Sovietov (Soviet Wings) and was perfect as the first Soviet export to the NHL. He was a decent player, but not a superstar that the Russians would miss in international action. He played 46 games for Calgary between 1989 and 1991, but is remembered mostly for his historic move to North American hockey.

5.10   D. Lars-Erik Sjoberg of the Winnipeg Jets

Before the Winnipeg Jets crashed, burned and resurrected in the desert as the Phoenix Coyotes, they, more than any other team, developed the first European–North American link in hockey. Lars-Erik Sjoberg, a 30-year-old veteran Swedish defenseman, was among the first Europeans attracted by Winnipeg. He played six seasons with the Jets, five in the WHA and his last, 1979–80, as an NHLer when the two leagues merged. Unlike other early arrivals to the NHL, Sjoberg's experience on European ice prepared him well for NHL hockey. He became the Jets' captain in 1975, leading the European-stocked team with as many as nine expatriates in the lineup—including Bobby Hull's linemates Anders Hedberg and Ulf Nilsson—to three Avco World Trophies in four years. When Winnipeg became an NHL franchise in 1979, Sjoberg became the league's first European-trained team captain.

5.11 B. Pelle Lindbergh of Sweden

Pelle Lindbergh's rise to NHL prominence as Philadelphia's starting netminder in 1982–83 began at the 1979 World Junior Championships, where he was named best goaltender and a member of the All-Star Team. Over the next couple of years he gained a world of experience, first at the World Championships, followed by his Olympic debut at Lake Placid in 1980 and, then, the Canada Cup in 1981. In his fourth NHL season, 1984–85, the Swedish marvel blossomed into the league's top goalie leading the Flyers to a 40–17–7 record and besting the high-flying Edmonton Oilers in regular-season standings 113 to 109 points. Although the Oilers defeated the Flyers for the Cup that year, Lindbergh's mobility and lightning-quick reflexes proved his worth as he out-balloted Buffalo's Tom Barrasso for the top honour bestowed on a NHL goalie, the Vezina Trophy. It was the first time a non-North American netminder won the award. Only months later, the 26-year-old Lindbergh died in a high-speed, alcohol-related car crash in New Jersey.

5.12 C. 1997–98

In 1997–98, with Wayne Gretzky in his 19th season, Mario Lemieux retired, Paul Kariya injured and only a few other North American scoring stars, such as Eric Lindros and John LeClair, in the race, the NHL witnessed its first trio of Europeans sweep the top scoring positions. Jaromir Jagr won the Art Ross Trophy as the leading point earner, followed by runners-up Peter Forsberg and Pavel Bure, who tied Gretzky with 90 points but finished third overall based on his superior goal count. Their 1-2-3 finish remains the only time Europeans have so dominated the NHL scoring race.

The NHL's top five scoring leaders of 1997–98

PLAYER	TEAM	GP	G	A	PTS	COUNTRY
Jaromir Jagr	Pittsburgh	77	35	67	102	Czech Rep.
Peter Forsberg	Colorado	72	25	66	91	Sweden
Pavel Bure	Vancouver	82	51	39	90	Russia
Wayne Gretzky	NYR	82	23	67	90	Canada
John LeClair	Philadelphia	82	51	36	87	USA

5.13 B. Finland

Although Finland has had a hard time winning gold medals among hockey's elite nations, their program cannot be faulted for its lack of star-quality NHLers. Among the best are Teemu Selanne and Saku Koivu, but the most successful NHL Finn remains Jari Kurri, who won five Stanley Cups between 1984 and 1990 as Wayne Gretzky's scoring partner on the Edmonton Oilers. Kurri first made waves at the 1978 European Junior Championships when he scored a double overtime winner in the gold-medal game versus the Soviet Union. Two years later, he played in the 1980 Olympics and, months after that, Edmonton's coach and general manger Glen Sather picked him 69th overall in the NHL Entry Draft. In his first 15 games of 1980–81, Kurri potted five goals, then, on November 26, his 16th NHL match, Sather finally paired the rookie right winger with Wayne Gretzky. On that historic night, Kurri scored a hat trick, two on assists by No. 99. Their combined magic on ice together earned Kurri four consecutive 50-goal seasons, including the NHL's first by a European—a 52-goal effort in 1983–84.

5.14 A. The Winnipeg Jets

While a few European-born players such as Stan Mikita and Bob Nystrom have had their jerseys retired, Thomas Steen of the Winnipeg Jets was the first to receive this honour among players taught in Europe. Steen played several years on two of Sweden's better clubs, Leksand and Farjestad, before Winnipeg selected him 103rd overall in the 1979 Entry Draft. A career Jet, Steen scored 264 goals and 817 points in 14 seasons; while his 553 career assists remains a record for the Winnipeg/Phoenix franchise. Upon his retirement in 1994, Steen's No. 25 jersey was hung from the rafters of Winnipeg Arena, a tribute bestowed previously on only one other Jets player: Bobby Hull.

5.15 B. Dominik Hasek of Czechoslovakia

Despite the emergence of many great imports backstopping NHL clubs during the 1990s, the first starting goalie with European training to win the Stanley Cup was Dominik Hasek. Quirky and unpredictable, Hasek developed his fleet-footedness playing goal in soccer in his hometown of Pardubice. After establishing himself as his country's top-ranking goalie, he made his first North American appearances representing Czechoslovakia at the 1984 and 1987 Canada Cups and the 1988 Olympics in Calgary. Hasek also participated in every World Championship—beginning in his NHL draft year, 1983, when Chicago picked him 207th overall—until he joined the NHL for good, seven years later in 1990. However, the Czechoslovak star's NHL transition wasn't easy, playing in only 25 games for the Blackhawks during two seasons of mop-up work behind Ed Belfour. His subsequent trade to Buffalo gave Hasek the chance to be number one and he took full advantage, mesmerizing shooters with an unorthodox sprawling style that looked a little like Ken Dryden's and a lot like no one else's. He was nimble, acrobatic and Gumby-like, contorting himself into Cirque du Soleil positions to stop the puck with every part of his body, including his head, soccer-style. When Hasek won consecutive Hart Trophies as league MVP in 1997 and 1998, he became the first goalie ever awarded multiple Harts and the first back-to-back winner since Wayne Gretzky in 1986 and 1987. During his second MVP-winning season of 1997–98, he stormed the 26-team NHL, zeroing a league-record 11 different teams in a 13-shutout season. His first Stanley Cup, and the first by a European starter, came in 2002 with Detroit. By then, Hasek was 37 years old.

5.16 C. The New York Islanders

The Islanders might not be the first team that comes to mind as a pursuer of European talent, but the club owns a few important NHL firsts in this category. On November 1, 1977, Sweden's Goran Hogosta became the first European-trained goalie to play in an NHL game when he replaced the injured Billy Smith for nine minutes in a shared 9–0 shutout against the Atlanta Flames. Then,

Czech Dominik Hasek becomes the first European-trained starting netminder to win the Stanley Cup after eliminating the Carolina Hurricanes at Detroit's Joe Louis Arena in 2002.

when the Islanders won the Stanley Cup in 1980, defenseman Stefan Persson and forward Anders Kallur were on board, to become the first European-trained players with their names etched on hockey's most cherished award. In fact, Person and Kallur were part of all four Islander championships between 1980 and 1983, making them the first non-North Americans with multiple Cups. Later, fellow Swede Tomas Jonsson joined the duo for the 1982 Cup, and when the club won their fourth in 1983, Mats Hallin made it a quartet of Europeans on the dynasty from Long Island.

5.17   A. The Montreal Canadiens in 1993

It's hard to imagine a European not playing a part on a Stanley Cup-winning team in today's NHL, but since the New York Islanders hoisted the first Cup sporting two Swedes in 1980, the Montreal Canadiens are the only team to have become champions without a European-trained player in the lineup. In 1993, the Habs did it with 24 Canadians and three Americans on the roster; and of those from Canada, fourteen came from Quebec and another seven from the Prairie provinces, which roughly resembled the makeup of Montreal great dynasties of the 1950s, 1960s and 1970s. Interestingly, Oleg Petrov of Moscow was a member of the 1992–93 Canadiens, but he never got his name on Lord Stanley's jug, because he hadn't played enough games to officially qualify as a Cup winner.

5.18   D. In 15 wins

From the moment Scotty Bowman entered the NHL, he showed a willingness to experiment with European players. In 1969, he became the first general manager to draft a European in Tommi Salmalainen, who was chosen 66th overall by St. Louis. But his greatest ploy came during the 1990s when he combined a couple of Russian veterans and that country's next generation of stars into the five-man unit of Sergei Fedorov, Vyacheslav Kozlov, Igor Larionov, Vladimir Konstantinov and Viacheslav Fetisov. The fivesome underperformed to great criticism during the club's 1996 playoff run, but no one complained about the quintet's play the following year. The Russians scored nine of the Wings' 16 goals in Detroit's upset of the defending-champion Colorado Avalanche in the Western Conference finals. All told, Detroit's playoff record was a dazzling 15–0 when at least one of its Russians registered at least a point. The only victory without a Russian point was the 2–1 Cup-clincher versus the Flyers. After the game, Larionov said, "I've been playing professional hockey for 20 years and this is the happiest moment in my life. We've got five Russians and I've heard every player gets the Cup for two days. Five times two equals 10 days. So we can take it to Russia for the Russian people to enjoy it, to touch it."

5.19 B. Alexei Kovalev of the New York Rangers

Pavel Bure and Alexei Kovalev. Between these two Russian puck maestros with the puzzling personalities, it was Bure's light who shined brightest in the NHL. But Kovalev won the 1994 Stanley Cup as New York defeated the Bure-led Canucks and became the first Russian scorer in the Cup finals with a goal at 8:29 of the third period of Game 1. Bure netted his marker just a little more than a game later at 1:03 of the first period in Game 3. Although Igor Kravchuk was the first former Soviet player to appear in a Cup finals match with Chicago in 1992, he did not score. Alexei Zhitnik of the Kings was the first ex-Soviet to post a point in the finals, an assist on a Luc Robitaille goal in the 1993 Cup showdown.

5.20 D. The Boston Bruins

If Matti Hagman is remembered at all today by NHL fans, it is probably due to his two-year stint as second-line centre behind Wayne Gretzky on the Edmonton Oilers of the early 1980s. Hagman was the "other" Finn forward on the Oilers after fellow countryman Jari Kurri. But Hagman was clearly no Kurri, although, by virtue of his age, he did precede Kurri as the first Finn to crack the NHL after his draft by Boston in 1975. He quickly impressed Bruins boss Harry Sinden at the 1976 Canada Cup, both for his offense, with six points in five games, and for his toughness, when he bounced Bobby Orr around on one particular forecheck. Hagman went on to play 75 games for Boston in 1976–77 and another eight playoff matches, including a contest on May 7, 1977, to become the first European-trained player in the Cup finals. He registered no points and Boston was swept by Montreal. After one more season split between the NHL and WHA, Hagman returned to Finland. But his NHL career wasn't over and he joined Gretzky's Oilers for a pair of 20-goal seasons between 1980 and 1982. After that, he stuck to the international game and became IFK Helsinki's leading scorer for several seasons.

5.21 A. Anders Hedberg of the New York Rangers in 1979

The first European to net a goal in Stanley Cup finals history is Anders Hedberg, one half of a pair of Swedes—the other was Ulf Nilsson—plucked from the WHA Winnipeg Jets in free agent signings by New York in June 1978. Hedberg and Nilsson brought New York style and skill, and a chance—after a seven-year Rangers absence from the final—at the Cup in 1979. Unfortunately, New York, with a surprise semi-final victory over the up-and-coming Islanders, met the powerhouse Montreal Canadiens in the final round. The Rangers took Game 1 but never won another match. Hedberg scored his historic goal against Ken Dryden in the second game, a 6–2 loss on May 15. Meanwhile, the first European with a Stanley Cup winner is German defenseman Uwe Krupp, who gave Colorado the Cup on a third-period overtime goal in 1996.

5.22 C. Borje Salming of Sweden

The NHL's early experiment with Europeans is littered with homesick players who faced myriad challenges, including the grind of an 80-game schedule, the intimidation and physical play, and the adjustment to North American culture and language. What many brought in skill, they lacked in brawn, which was usually their downfall, with most either getting demoted after a three-game trial or giving up within a season or two of their ill-fated arrival. NHL general managers were keen to exploit this fresh source of talent, but never knew what to expect from a late-round pick or free-agent signing, no matter how good his European numbers. Then came Borje Salming in 1973. Billed as a rushing defenseman with big speed and stickhandling skills, Salming broke the stereotype of the infamous "Chicken Swede" label by taking on all challengers, including the day's best brawlers such as Dave Schultz. He took more punishment than his peers had to, but he showed that Europeans could survive as stars in the NHL. Salming played a combined 1,148 games for Toronto and Detroit and is one of only a handful of players from outside North American to have gained entry into the Hockey Hall of Fame. The tribute was bestowed

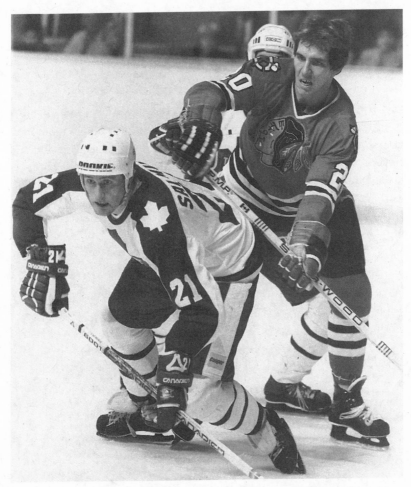

Sweden's Borje Salming pioneered the way for other Europeans in the NHL by battling each game against such foes as Al Secord of the Chicago Blackhawks.

in 1996, several years after Vladislav Trekiak became the first European star elected to the Hall in 1989. However, Tretiak never played in the NHL, so the honour among European-NHLers belongs to Salming, the six-time all-star blueliner, who changed the complexion of NHL hockey by paving the way for other European talent. Two years after Salming's Hall selection, Peter Stastny was inducted in his first year of eligibility.

Storming the NHL

FOR A GUY WHO admitted, "I really didn't plan to stay here that long," Teppo Numminen has had quite an NHL career. The Finnish rearguard figured on playing a year or two, only to stay 20-plus seasons and, on November 13, 2006, set the league record for most games played by a European-trained player when he surpassed fellow countryman Jari Kurri's mark by skating in his 1,252nd match. In this game, match up the players and the NHL records they hold either among fellow Europeans or all NHLers.

Solutions are on page 139

Alexander Ovechkin   Nicklas Lidstrom   Dominik Hasek
Sergei Fedorov   Alexander Mogilny   Paul Stastny
Jaromir Jagr   Jari Kurri   Peter Forsberg
Teemu Selanne   Peter/Anton Stastny   Evgeni Nabokov

1. _____ Most shots by a European in one regular season

2. _____ Most points by a European in one regular-season game

3. _____ Most shutouts by a European goalie in one regular season

4. _____ Most goals by a European in one regular season

5. _____ Most goals by an NHL rookie in one regular season

6. _____ Longest consecutive point-scoring streak by an NHL rookie

7. _____ Most games by a European goalie in one regular season

8. _____ Most points by a European in one period in a regular-season game

9. _____ Most overtime points by an NHL player in a career

10. _____ Most goals by a European right winger in a career

11. _____ Most overtime assists by a European in a career

12. _____ Most goals by an NHL player in one playoff year

6

THE OLYMPIANS

AMONG THE MANY SPECTACULAR plays at the 2002 Olympics was an inspirational Mario Lemieux move that led to Canada's first goal in the gold-medal game against USA. Behind 1–0 to the Americans late in the first period, Chris Pronger appeared to feed a pass to a streaking Lemieux. But the Canadian captain let the puck go through his legs to Paul Kariya who had the open net to tie the game. Mike Richter, who was sensational in nets for USA, viewed the play this way: "I can see them both there, and the pass goes practically to Mario's stick. He doesn't just *not* play it, he actually puts his stick there to play it, then moves his stick. It was a beautiful play, and a play you have to honour as a goalie. Obviously I honoured it a bit too much," said Richter. In our final chapter, we light the flame to celebrate the swifter, higher and stronger athletes of Olympic hockey.

Answers are on page 119

6.1 What is the most number of medals won by a player in men's Olympic hockey?
   A. Three medals
   B. Four medals
   C. Five medals
   D. Six medals

6.2 Who scored the winning goal in USA's 4–3 victory against the Soviets at the 1980 Olympics?
   A. Mark Pavelich
   B. Dave Christian
   C. Neal Broten
   D. Mike Eruzione

6.3 At that fateful Olympic game in 1980 between USA and the Soviet Union, famed Soviet coach Viktor Tikhonov made a decision that he later regarded as the biggest mistake of his career. What did he do?

A. He went with five defensemen instead of six in the lineup

B. He made a line-change error, causing his team to be assessed a too-many-men-on-the-ice penalty, which led to the winning goal

C. He pulled goalie Vladislav Tretiak after the first period

D. He broke up his famed five-man offense-defense units

6.4 Besides 1980, in which other Olympic Games did the United States win a gold medal in hockey?

A. In 1932 at Lake Placid, USA

B. In 1952 at Oslo, Norway

C. In 1960 at Squaw Valley, USA

D. In 1972 at Sapporo, Japan

6.5 Which country won a surprising gold medal in hockey at the 1936 Olympics?

A. Great Britain

B. France

C. Czechoslovakia

D. USA

6.6 Which Olympic Games was the first to have almost full participation of NHL players?

A. The 1992 Olympics in Albertville, France

B. The 1994 Olympics in Lillehammer, Norway

C. The 1998 Olympics in Nagano, Japan

D. The 2002 Olympics in Salt Lake City, USA

6.7 At what age did the oldest player participate in Olympic hockey?

A. 36 years old

B. 40 years old

C. 44 years old

D. 48 years old

6.8 Which coach was accused of tanking a game during the 2006 Olympics?

 A. Pat Quinn of Canada
 B. Bengt-Ake Gustafsson of Sweden
 C. Vladimir Krikunov of Russia
 D. Erkka Westerlund of Finland

6.9 Who is Vsevolod Bobrov?

 A. A two-sport Olympian
 B. The Soviet coach at the 1972 Summit Series
 C. The first captain of the Soviet national team
 D. All of the above

6.10 After winning the gold medal at their first Olympic Games in 1956, the Soviet Union went on to lose only to the USA (1960 and 1980) and which other country in the next nine Olympic tournaments until 1992?

 A. Sweden
 B. Canada
 C. Czechoslovakia
 D. No other country, the Soviets only lost to USA

6.11 Which goalie lost to the Czech Republic's Dominik Hasek in a dramatic semi-final shootout that eliminated Canada from gold-medal contention in 1998?

 A. Ed Balfour
 B. Patrick Roy
 C. Martin Brodeur
 D. Curtis Joseph

6.12 Prior to their gold in 2002, when was the last time Canada had a first-place finish in Olympic hockey?

 A. 14 years
 B. 22 years
 C. 38 years
 D. 50 years

6.13 Before the 2002 Olympics began, icemaker Trent Evans buried what object for good luck under the ice at Salt Lake City's E Center?

A. A silver horseshoe
B. A rabbit's foot
C. A miniature Stanley Cup
D. A Canadian dollar coin

6.14 Prior to its gold-medal loss to Canada in 2002, when was the last time an American men's hockey team lost on home ice at the Olympics?

A. 1932
B. 1960
C. 1980
D. 2002

6.15 In what year was women's hockey first played at the Olympic level?

A. 1992
B. 1994
C. 1998
D. 2002

6.16 Who was the gold-medal–winning goalie for USA at the 1980 Olympics?

A. Pete LoPresti
B. Jim Craig
C. Steve Janaszak
D. Jack McCartan

6.17 Which NHL goalie "played the role" of the USA goalie for the action scenes in *Miracle*, the feature-length film about the 1980 US Olympic gold-medal win in men's hockey?

A. Jim Craig
B. Tom Barrasso
C. Bill Ranford
D. Chris Osgood

6.18 What is the most number of Winter Olympics participated in by a player who also played in the NHL?

A. Two Olympics
B. Four Olympics

   ✗ C. Six Olympics

      D. Eight Olympics

6.19 Which Canadian goalie lost the shootout that handed Sweden its first Olympic gold medal in 1994 and subsequently refused to allow his likeness to appear on a Swedish postage stamp celebrating the winning goal?

      A. Manny Legace

      B. Sean Burke

      C. Trevor Kidd

   ✗ D. Corey Hirsch

6.20 Who coached USA to their Olympic gold-medal performance in 1980?

   ✗ A. Herb Brooks

      B. Paul Holmgren

      C. Lou Nanne

      D. Bob Johnson

6.21 Herb Brooks, coach of the gold-medal-winning U.S. Olympic team in 1980, had a playing career with which league?

      A. The old International Hockey League

   ✗ B. The United States Hockey League

      C. The World Hockey Association

      D. The National Hockey League

6.22 Which goalie gave up a fluke goal to Belarus during the quarter-finals and eliminated his powerhouse team from medal contention at the 2002 Olympics?

      A. Nikolai Khabibulin of Russia

   ✗ B. Tommy Salo of Sweden

      C. Jussi Markkanen of Finland

      D. Dominik Hasek of the Czech Republic

6.23 In what position did Canada finish at the 2006 Olympics?

      A. Second place (silver)

      B. Third place (bronze)

      C. Fifth place

   ✗ D. Seventh place

6.24 What is the record for most goals by one player in one Olympic tournament?
A. Seven goals
B. 17 goals
C. 27 goals
X D. 37 goals

6.25 Prior to 2010, how many players belong to the Triple Gold Club, with a Stanley Cup and gold medals in the World Championships and Olympics?
A. 18 players
X B. 22 players
C. 26 players
D. 30 players

6.26 How many goals did Canada's women score and allow in their Olympic gold-medal showing in 2006?
A. 26 goals scored; 22 goals allowed
B. 33 goals scored; 15 goals allowed
C. 39 goals scored; nine goals allowed
X D. 46 goals scored; two goals allowed

6.27 How much did a private bidder pay in 2003 for the puck used in USA's game-winning goal against the Soviets at the 1980 Olympics?
A. Between US$1,000 and US$4,000
B. Between US$4,000 and US$8,000
C. Between US$8,000 and US$12,000
X D. More than US$12,000

6.28 Who is the only player to have won gold medals at the Olympics, World Championships and World Junior Championships and titles in the Stanley Cup, World Cup of Hockey and Memorial Cup?
A. Joe Sakic
B. Mario Lemieux
X C. Scott Niedermayer
D. Steve Yzerman

The Olympians

6.1 B. Four medals

After the 2010 Winter Games in Vancouver, a few more players may share this career record, but presently the mark is held by legendary Soviet goalie Vladislav Tretiak, with three golds and a silver between 1972 and 1984; defenseman Igor Kravchuk, who played on three teams—the Soviet Union in 1988, the Unified Team in 1992 and Russia in 1998 and 2002—to win two golds, one silver and one bronze; and Jiri Holik, the durable left winger, who won two silvers and two bronzes with Czechoslovakia from 1964 to 1976. Each man can expect to make room on the podium as a number of three-time Olympic medalists could earn their fourth in 2010, including Saku Koivu of Finland (1994, 1998 and 2006) and Robert Lang of the Czech Republic (1992, 1998 and 2006). So which hockey player has gone the longest time between earning medals at the Olympics? Little-known forward Richard Torriana played for the Swiss national squad at age 16 during the 1928 Winter Games in his hometown of St. Moritz and helped Switzerland claim the bronze medal. Then 20 years later, Torriana notched another third-place finish at the 1948 Winter Games (where he was also the official torch bearer) to bookend his international career. To date, Torriana is only equalled among all Olympians by American John Heaton, who won silvers in the skeleton in 1928 and 1948.

6.2 D. Mike Eruzione

Before being named captain of the 1980 US Olympic team, Mike Eruzione starred for Boston University and, later, moved to the Toledo Goaldiggers of the International Hockey League, where he won the rookie of the year award and the Turner Cup championship in 1978. Then, on February 22, 1980, at the Olympic Center in Lake Placid, New York, the amateur hockey player's life changed forever when he fired a snapshot from outside the slot in the third period and beat Vladimir Myshkin for the go-ahead goal against the powerhouse Soviet Union. With exactly 10 minutes remaining, the Americans seized the moment, kept the Soviets from scoring and hung on for the 4–3 win, making Eruzione's winning goal one of the most played highlights in American sports. In March 2008, it was voted the greatest sports highlight of all time by ESPN viewers.

6.3   C. He pulled goalie Vladislav Tretiak after the first period

Much has been made of the Americans' stunning 4–3 victory over the Soviets at the 1980 Olympics, but how much did coach Viktor Tikhonov's goalie substitution influence the game's outcome? If you ask Tikhonov, the most successful coach in international hockey, this blunder was the biggest mistake he ever made. With just a second remaining in period one, Vladislav Tretiak stopped Dave Christian's shot but gave up a rebound to Mark Johnson, who evened the game 2–2. Tikhonov was so infuriated that he pulled his star goalie and installed Vladimir Myshkin between the pipes. After two periods, the Soviets had pulled ahead 3–2, but USA marched back in the third with two goals. So how huge was his mistake really? You can be sure if the Soviets had won, and they should have playing with either Tretiak or Myshkin, Tikhonov would never have ranked it his greatest error of judgment.

6.4   C. In 1960 at Squaw Valley, USA

Somehow it just doesn't seem fair. Despite winning the gold medal under arguably more challenging circumstances, the 1960 US Olympic hockey squad remains forever in the shadow of the much flashier "Miracle on Ice" team of 1980. For the seldom-remembered gold medalists of Squaw Valley in 1960, there were no sweet endorsement deals, film adaptations, fat NHL contracts or catchy nicknames. Yet these amateurs had to beat the four best teams in the world for their first-place finish, a greater achievement than that of their 1980 counterparts, who defeated just two teams in the final round. For the 1960 Americans, it began with two successive wins in the preliminary round robin matches. In the next seven days of the pool finals, they mowed down five teams, first with a convincing 6–3 win against the Swedes, then a routine 9–1 stomp over an out-matched German squad. Many believed the next contest against the world champion Canadians would determine the gold. USA chiselled out a 2–1 win as goalie Jack McCartan stopped 39 of 40 shots, compared to just 27 faced

Team USA's historic "miracle" win against the mighty Soviet Union at the 1980 Olympic Games on February 22 at Lake Placid, N.Y. The Americans then defeated Finland to capture Olympic gold.

by Don Head of Canada. The Americans were sitting pretty for a top podium place but still needed two more victories. Down 2–1 against the Soviet Union after 20 minutes in the next contest, Bill Christian stepped into the hero's spotlight and scored twice to hand USA another stunning win, their fourth straight. Their own miracle at hand, the 1960 US squad finally crushed Czechoslovakia 9–4 to claim America's first Olympic gold in hockey. For whatever reason, the sweetness of that original success is all but lost, consumed in the breadth of celebration after America's second gold of 1980. Here's another trivia nugget: After his Olympic success, McCartan made it to the NHL, only to survive eight games with the New York Rangers. But it was long enough for him to become the very first Olympic goalie to backstop an NHL team.

6.5 A. Great Britain

It may be the greatest upset by a gold medalist in Olympic hockey history. The 1936 Winter Olympics in Garmisch-Partenkirchen, Germany, were supposed to deliver podium results for Canada same as those in 1920, 1924, 1928 and 1932: another gold medal. Canada was represented by the Port Arthur Bearcats, the western finalists for the 1935 Allan Cup, awarded for senior amateur supremacy in Canada. At the time, the world hadn't caught up to Canada in hockey. Its teams were near invincible, as almost any squad of skilled Canadians could come home victorious from Europe. In fact, prior to the 1936 Games, Canada had lost only one international match of any significance, that to the USA in the 1933 World Championships. Further, in four previous Olympics, Canadian squads proved themselves so superior, they decimated their opponents in 17 games by a cumulative tally of 209 goals to eight. Ironically, the 1936 British team was stocked with Canadian players who had been born in Britain, including Jimmy Foster, a Scottish-born Canadian netminder considered among the finest in his day. When Canada found out about Foster's (and other players) inclusion, they protested and the IIHF conceded in Canada's favour. But Canada, in a show of Olympic spirit, withdrew its opposition days later. It was a decision that would haunt Canada as Foster proved to be the difference, leading Britain to defeat his former country 2–1 in the semi-final pools. The Canadians expected to get another crack at the British squad in the final, but Olympic officials overturned the original rules (under which all teams thought they were playing by) and ruled that because Britain had beaten Canada once, a return match wasn't necessary. In the finals the Brits guaranteed their gold with two shutouts by Foster, 5–0 against Czechoslovakia and a 0–0 tie versus the US. It was almost inconceivable that Canada wouldn't win the title, but they finished the tournament 7–1–0, better than Great Britain's 5–0–2 record but not good enough for the gold medal by Olympic standards of the day.

6.6   C. The 1998 Olympics in Nagano, Japan

Although NHLers started playing in the World Championships in 1977, league participation at the Olympic level only began at Nagano in 1998. Several key events led to NHL players being eligible for *both* competitions. The first came in 1977 when the IIHF brought Canada back into international play (after seven years of protest by Hockey Canada) by allowing NHLers whose teams had been eliminated from the Stanley Cup playoffs to participate in the World Championships. This became possible because the timing of the Worlds coincided with the NHL playoffs each spring, compared to the Winter Games, which were every four years in February, deep into the regular season. League officials and team owners were loathe to free up their best players and risk injury for an Olympic competition that had no benefit to their franchise leading up to the playoffs. But after the NHL lockout eliminated half of the 1994—95 season, the new collective bargaining agreement committed both players and the league to the 1998 Olympics, which would boost worldwide promotion of the game. The league also had an eye towards 2002, with the Olympics on home turf in Salt Lake City, Utah. As a result, each side made compromises for Nagano, which included an NHL shut down for 17 days and a reformatted IIHF playing schedule to accommodate for travel fatigue. Some 14 countries played in two distinct rounds with many national teams, heavy in NHLers, participating in the later series of elimination matches. The product delivered excellent hockey as the Czech Republic's netminder Dominik Hasek stoned Canada in a tense semi-final shootout and then held off the Russians for the gold medal. Television ratings and general interest were so high that NHL involvement became standard in Olympic competition.

6.7   D. 48 years old

When the US Olympic team iced its 23-man roster at Palasport Olimpico in Turin, Italy, for the 2006 Winter Games, defenseman Chris Chelios had made the cut at age 44. Although he set the record for the longest time between first and last Olympics at 22 years, he was still only the seventh-oldest hockey player in Games history. At the time, an elated Chelios said, "If we have success, maybe they'll ask me back a fifth time." The Americans finished a disappointing eighth overall in 2006, and Chelios is unlikely to get another invite, even though he played in his 25th NHL season in 2008–09. If he returns in 2010, the Detroit defenseman will be 48 years old and the same age as Hungarian Bela Ordody and German Alfred Steinka, the oldest hockey players in Olympic history. Ordody and Steinka competed at the age of 48 in the 1928 Olympics in St. Moritz. Germany and Hungary finished in 10th and 11th place overall during that tournament.

6.8   B. Bengt-Ake Gustafsson of Sweden

Considering that Sweden won the gold medal, the strategy, if that's what it was, paid off handsomely for them. Did the Swedes intentionally lose a game to Slovakia in the round robin in order to duck the Czech Republic or Canada and play lowly Switzerland for an easier ride into the medal rounds? The evidence is damning. *Before* the 3–0 defeat to Slovakia, Bengt-Ake Gustafsson said: "It's difficult. As it looks right now, we will be facing Switzerland. But if we win we can get the Czechs or Canada. And, of course, it is the question: Shall we win or shall we play a good game to get a 0–0 result?" After the IIHF expressed concern over his comments, Gustafsson backtracked saying, "You've got to try to save your energy for the next game, which is the important one... That's all I said... perhaps I said too much, I don't know." The powerhouse Swedes, who were outshot 31–17 by Slovakia, then went on to beat in succession Switzerland 6–2, the Czech Republic 7–3 and Finland 3–2 for the gold.

6.9   D. All of the above

By every qualification, Vsevolod Bobrov was a natural. A gifted multi-talented athlete and the original Russian Rocket, Bobrov first trained in soccer and bandy, the stick-and-ball game played on ice that was sometimes called "Russian hockey." His first contact with the puck version of the sport came in 1945 while touring with the Soviet national soccer club in Great Britain, where he saw North American-style hockey being played by Canadian teams on tour. His interest became so great, that shortly after playing soccer for the USSR at the 1952 Helsinki Olympics (where he scored a hat trick in one legendary game against Yugoslavia), he quit and dedicated his skills entirely to his winter sport. He was named the first captain of the Soviet national hockey team and won best forward honours at the World Championships in 1954, when the Soviet Union upset Canada with a shocking 7–2 gold-medal victory. Two years later, at Cortina, Italy, Bobrov played hero again and helped the Soviets win gold in their first Olympic tournament, by scoring nine goals in seven games to end Canada's domination at that event. Upon his retirement the following year, he had a lifetime record of 89 goals in 59 international games. He had several highlights in his coaching career, including the historic Summit Series against Canada in 1972.

6.10   D. No other country, the Soviets only lost to USA

After the 1920 Antwerp Olympics put hockey on the international map, at last three hockey eras dominated future Winter Games. With the exception of 1936, Canada owned Olympic gold with six first-place showings until 1956 when the Soviet Union stunned Canada's representatives, the Kitchener-Waterloo Dutchmen, in a 2–0 gold-medal match. It was a devastating result for the Canadians, and their worst performance internationally with an uncharacteristic bronze medal after USA beat Czechoslovakia 9–4 for the silver. The game proved to be a turning point during Canada's last days of hockey dominance. It also ushered in the Canada-USSR rivalry and a new era of world supremacy as the Soviet team crushed their opponents every four years between 1956 and 1992, except for the miracle upsets of 1960 and 1980 by USA. Their four-decade-long gold streak finally ended with the political breakup of the USSR in 1991, although the team that represented the new Russia at the 1992 Albertville Olympics played a traditional Soviet-style game. Without the famous lettering

"CCCP" on their jerseys, they still won gold. Since then, another Olympic era has evolved with a more balanced, open tournament where any of the top six nations are gold-medal contenders.

6.11 B. Patrick Roy

There were never really any other favourites for the gold medal than Canada at the 1998 Olympics. For the first time in history, each country was represented by their best players and Canada iced a Hall of Fame line-up in Wayne Gretzky, Ray Bourque, Steve Yzerman, Joe Sakic and Patrick Roy. The Czech Republic had, well, Dominik Hasek, who almost single-handedly carried his team and country to victory. Or at least it seemed that way, as Hasek gave up just six goals on 135 shots throughout the event. "The Dominator" was in absolute control, backstopping a Czech squad with only 11 NHLers (fewest among the top Olympic nations) but sporting a disciplined two-way game built on a defense-first philosophy that had teammate Jaromir Jagr joking, "Next time write 68D next to my name," in reference to the offensive star's commitment to defense. As the tournament progressed, both teams played to expectations until their semi-final match-up. From the opening face-off, it was a classic goaltender's duel, pitting net giants Hasek and Roy against each other through 60 minutes of regulation time, but not before some last minute dramatics when Roy was pulled for the sixth at-tacker and Trevor Linden scored to tie the game 1–1. Another 10 minutes of overtime settled nothing, as Canada fired five shots at Hasek, compared to the one shot Roy handled against the Czechs. The shootout would have to decide the finalist for the gold-medal game. Each side selected five shooters and, inexplicably, Canada's coach Marc Crawford left Wayne Gretzky on the bench. Robert Reichel skated in first and fired a wrist shot to Roy's stick-side. "I was waiting, waiting and I saw a little spot," said Reichel, whose NHL record on penalty shots was a perfect two for two. Reichel's shot pinged off the post and into the net. St. Patrick foiled the rest of the Czech shooters, but as good as Roy was, Hasek was better— he blocked all five Canadian shots. Eric Lindros, Canada's third marksman, had the best chance. He faked Hasek cleanly, but his shot hit the post. Brendan Shanahan, who shot fifth, was Canada's last hope. He missed too, and after the game apologized for "letting the country down." Canada had come to the Olympics to win gold and there was no second prize in their mindset. When it was all over, Gretzky hung his head on the Canadian bench. "This is the worst feeling in the world right now," he said.

6.12   D. 50 years

It's a little difficult to understand how a so-called hockey superpower could fall victim to an Olympic gold drought of 50 years, but Canada's half-century absence from a top-place finish is one of the unfortunate stories in the development of international hockey. So what happened to the Canadian game in that period of time between 1952 when the Edmonton Mercurys won gold and 2002, the next time another team of Canucks stepped up to the podium and heard "O Canada" in 2002? As we discussed in Chapter 4, the simple answer is that for most of five decades, Canada's best players weren't participating at the "amateur" level of the Olympics and World Championships, while European countries developed hockey programs and leagues specifically to stock their national clubs with their top talent. The first Olympics with a truly level playing field came with full NHL participation in 1998. Canada finished out of medal contention that year, but on February 24, 2002, exactly 50 years to day after the Edmonton Mercurys won Canada's last Olympic gold medal, another Canadian team faced-off for gold. Their opponent was a powerful American squad marking its own anniversary, 22 years and two days removed from its historic "Miracle on Ice" victory in 1980. Led by executive director Wayne Gretzky, Canada celebrated what proved to be a truly golden anniversary.

6.13   D. A Canadian dollar coin

In a now-celebrated story, Canadian icemaker Trent Evans secretly embedded a Canadian one-dollar loonie coin under the ice at the centre faceoff circle at the E Center in 2002. Evans realized that the rink had no centre dot to indicate where the officials should drop the puck. So he iced the lucky loonie to mark the spot and obscured it with a drop of yellow paint. Both Canadian teams were told but sworn to secrecy. When Canada's women won gold against USA the gambit was almost discovered when several Canuck players kissed and touched the ice covering the coin. Fortunately, "... the girls did a good job of keeping it secret," said Evans. After 20 days, 11 games and two gold medals, it was Wayne Gretzky, who, at a post-Olympic press scrum, pulled the coin from his jacket and revealed to the world Canada's hidden talisman, saying simply it was "for luck." "We took it out of the ice tonight and we're going to present it to the Hall of Fame. We got two gold medals out of it. That's pretty special," said Gretzky. Beneath the loonie, Evans also buried a Canadian dime, which he planned to keep as a souvenir.

6.14 A. 1932

American teams are virtually unbeatable on US ice. Before their heartbreaking 5–2 loss to Canada in February 2002, the Americans went undefeated at home with an amazing 21 wins, zero losses and three ties dating back to 1932. Their 70-year reign began at Lake Placid in 1932 after they lost a 2–1 overtime decision to Canada on February 4. They came back in the tournament and earned a 4–1–1 record and the silver medal. Then, at the 1960 Winter Games in Squaw Valley, the USA won its gold medal in hockey with a perfect 7–0–0. They repeated in 1980 at Lake Placid with 6–0–1 during its historic gold-medal performance. In 2002, the USA went 4–0–1 before its 5–2 defeat to Canada.

6.15 C. 1998

Olympic hockey has witnessed many defining moments, few as significant as what transpired at Nagano, Japan, in 1998. For the first time men's hockey had full-scale NHL participation and women's hockey was making its debut as a medal sport with six nations competing at this inaugural competition. As expected, in the women's competition, Canada and USA played for the gold, but the outcome proved a blow to the Canadians, who were the favourites after winning all four World Championships against the Americans. In the gold-medal game on February 17, USA played with new confidence, buoyed by their 7–4 upset over Canada three days earlier in the final game of round-robin play. That loss shocked the Canadians and they never recovered, losing 3–1 in their bid to win the first Olympic gold medal in women's hockey. A nice ending to the USA's triumph came when they were pictured on boxes of Wheaties, the cereal that has featured many great athletes since the 1930s when Johnny Weissmuller first endorsed "The Breakfast of Champions." "It's every Olympic athlete's dream. First a gold medal and then your own Wheaties box," said US captain Cammi Granato after appearing one of the most prestigious photoshoots in American sports culture.

6.16   B. Jim Craig

An All-American netminder at Boston University and linchpin for the Terriers' 1978 NCAA championship squad, Jim Craig was the unanimous choice as starting goalie of the 1980 US Olympic hockey team. At the Lake Placid Games, Craig put on a clinic of clutch netminding, defeating the highly favoured Soviet Union in the first medal round, then Finland for Olympic gold. Against the mighty Soviets, the Americans pulled off a minor miracle as Craig played the game of his life. Even though they were outshot 39–16, the North Easton, Massachusetts native made 36 saves, many in spectacular fashion, and his teammates scored four times in the dramatic 4–3 upset. So unpredictable and so transformative was the victory that in a sporting culture dominated by the larger-than-life accomplishments of such figures as Babe Ruth and Jesse Owens, Sports Illustrated selected the win by Craig and his college hockey scrubs as "the single most indelible moment in all of US sports history" and ranked their gold medal as the greatest sports moment of the 20th century.

6.17   C. Bill Ranford

In the Hollywood film Miracle, producers stocked the cast of the US team with several first-time actors, but Craig was played by Eddie Cahill and by NHL netminder Bill Ranford during the action sequences. "To add authenticity to the scenes, I tried duplicating some of Jim's signature moves," Ranford said. "I'd try to copy the way he played the puck with his glove hand near the bottom of his stick to help clear it out of the zone, or the way he'd hold his glove high on the crossbar so he could watch guys behind the net."

6.18   C. Six Olympics

Raimo Helminen may have been an NHLer, but his reputation as an elite player came at the international level. He played for Finland during a career that spanned almost two decades from the 1984 World Junior Championships, where he amassed an eye-popping

24 points in seven matches, to his final Olympics at 38 years old in 2002. During that time, Helminen won 10 of 11 medals earned by Finland in the Olympics and World Championships (that 11th was a silver at the Worlds in 1992). He may not be as well known as fellow countrymen Jari Kurri or Teemu Selanne, but he garnered several scoring titles in the Finnish leagues, established the all-time world record for national team games at 330 with Finland and became the first hockey player and just one of 11 athletes who share the all-time record of six Olympic starts, first achieved by bobsledder Karl-Erik Eriksson in 1984. Helminen's Olympic medal count includes three of the four medals won by Finland, with a silver at Calgary in 1988 and, later, two bronzes in 1994 and 1998. Helminen, known as a passer more than a shooter, tallied six goals and 24 points in 39 Olympic contests, only playing in 2002 because fellow countryman Saku Koivu was battling non-Hodgkin's lymphoma. In the NHL, Helminen played 117 games (13–46–59) for the New York Rangers, Minnesota North Stars and New York Islanders between 1985 and 1989.

6.19   D. Corey Hirsch

It is a goal that represents everything in hockey to Sweden. After 74 frustrating years of silver, bronze and early-round finishes, Sweden's golden hour came in dramatic fashion: a final round shootout featuring Peter Forsberg versus Canadian netminder Corey Hirsch. Sixty minutes of regulation play and another 10 minutes of overtime settled nothing with the 1994 gold-medal game deadlocked 2–2. In the shootout each team scored twice on their first four of five shots, leaving the fifth shooters, Forsberg and Paul Kariya to decide destiny. Forsberg rolled in on Hirsch, moved left, pulled the goalie with him and then slipped the puck from his forehand to his backhand and with one glove on his stick pushed the puck under the outstretched arm of Hirsch and into the open net. It was an inspired maneuver by the 20-year-old wunderkind of Swedish hockey, and after Tommy Salo's stop on Kariya at the other end, Sweden had its first Olympic gold. Many commemorative items honoured Forsberg's historic marker, including a Swedish postage stamp that took inspiration from Associated Press photographer Al Behrman's overhead shot of Hirsch being deked out. But there were a few differences in the

The Swedish postage stamp that celebrates Peter Forsberg's inventive 1994 gold-medal goal against Canada's Corey Hirsch in the dramatic shootout between the two Olympic finalists.

philatelic depiction of the play. Hirsch was so disgraced by the goal that he refused to allow his likeness to be used, a decision he later regretted. So Sweden cast their national hero triumphantly scoring on an unidentifiable goalie who wore a blue jersey instead of red, and No.11, instead of Hirsch's No. 1.

6.20 A. Herb Brooks

When television play-by-play man Al Michaels' said "Do you believe in miracles? Yes!" at the end of USA's stunning 4–3 win against the Soviets in 1980, he wasn't exaggerating the momentous event by much. At that moment in time, it was a miracle in hockey history. And as much as it had to do with sheer pluck and determination, it was attributable mostly to one man: coach Herb Brooks. Known for his bristly character and fanatical preparation, Brooks earned his reputation for winning at the University of Minnesota, where he led the Golden Gophers to three NCAA championships in the 1970s. How he convinced a bunch of college kids of the notion that if they try their best they might do the impossible and beat the unbeatable Soviets is considered one of the greatest coaching performances in American sports; and the most incredible sales job ever done on the minds of athletes who, according to hockey experts, won something that just never, ever should've been possible. The Soviets were stocked with veterans from 1972's legendary Summit Series clash against Canada, players such as Valeri Kharlamov, Vladimir Petrov, Vladislav Tretiak and with the next wave of Russian young guns, including Sergei Makarov and Vladimir Krutov. Meanwhile, similar to the Soviets, who devoted themselves exclusively to hockey (and were amateur in name only), Brooks spent 18 months putting together his roster, holding numerous tryouts and psychological tests before playing a grinding four-month schedule of exhibition games across Europe and North America. Built around a core of players that included future NHLers Neal Broten, Ken Morrow and Mike Ramsey, Brooks emphasized speed, conditioning and discipline to counter the skill of European and Canadian squads. He shaped his players by challenging them both physically and psychologically and making himself the common enemy, a ploy that had worked to perfection for Scotty Bowman's Stanley Cup triumphs with the Montreal Canadiens. Brooks also made several strategic moves before the Olympics, playing forward Dave Christian on defense for greater mobility and making each line competitive speed-wise with centres Broten, Mark Johnson and Mark Pavelich. And between the pipes, Jim Craig was coming into his own at just the right time, preventing the Soviets' equalizer after the Americans took the 4–3 lead for good. The victory against the Soviets came to define Olympic achievement, where anything is possible, even by miracle.

6.21 B. The United States Hockey League

A life-long coach, Herb Brooks had a playing career that included four years with the University of Minnesota Gophers between 1955 and 1959 and another three seasons in the USHL, the top junior hockey league in the mid-western United States. At the international level, he was a member of the U.S. national team during five World Championships and two Olympics, though he never skated as a regular, after being the final cut in 1960. But Brooks's own failure as a player unable to make the 1960 squad pushed him to succeed as a coach. When they won gold without him, Brooks and his father were at home in Minnesota. "I guess they cut the right guy," the old man said, devastating the younger Brooks. That moment of humiliation drove Brooks to coach three national championships at the University of Minnesota and, then, before a stunned hockey world, win the gold medal for USA at the 1980 Olympics.

6.22 B. Tommy Salo of Sweden

Perhaps the most unforgettable play of the 2002 Olympic tournament was an 80-foot slapshot unleashed by Belarus defenseman Vladimir Kopat with two minutes left in his country's championship-round game against Sweden. Goalie Tommy Salo bungled the high shot and the puck hit his mask, bounced over his head, rolled down his back and trickled across the goal line, giving Belarus a stunning 4–3 win. Kopat, a toiler in the Russian leagues, became a national hero overnight. "I could say I saw the goalie moving out and I decided to send the puck over and behind him, but that is a joke," smiled Kopat. "I just made a shot and willed it to make a goal." After going 3–0–0 in the preliminary round, the Swedes were eliminated, an upset of staggering proportions of one of the best Olympic teams. "When we ran out of time I couldn't believe it... I couldn't believe it was over," said Swedish forward Daniel Alfredsson. The Swedish tabloid *Expressen* ripped the lineup, publishing pictures of every player with his NHL salary underneath the headline: "Guilty of dishonouring their country."

6.23 D. Seventh place

Canada, the 2006 Olympic favourite, had depth at every position and a Wayne Gretzky-managed team that had captured gold in 2002. So what went wrong with US$94 million worth of NHL talent on his 2006 roster? There were criticisms of an absence of youth without the likes of Sidney Crosby, Dion Phaneuf or Eric Staal in the lineup, of a lack of leadership in captain Joe Sakic's reserved manner, of bad boy Todd Bertuzzi's selection and, finally, of Gretzky's own off-ice distractions with wife Janet being implicated in a gambling ring. But it really came down to team chemistry. Canada had simply failed to gel, getting shut out three times and going goalless in 11 of its last 12 periods of Olympic play. Still, Canada's final game was classic, a thrilling 2–0 nail-biter against its old rivals, Russia. "We still were relying on our individual skills and we just didn't get over that hump that we needed to get over," admitted coach Pat Quinn. Their seventh-place finish proved to be Canada's worst showing in Olympic history.

6.24   D. 37 goals

Was scoring sensation Harry Watson so good that he could score at will against any team or were Canada's opponents as weak as the scores indicated during the 1924 Olympics? In truth, Watson's superior puck skills bloated his totals against vastly inferior European clubs that were still in their formative hockey years. How else could he rack up 37 goals in five games and his team amass a goal-count margin of 110–3? To be honest, it wasn't fair pitting Watson's Toronto Granites, Canada's Allan Cup winners of 1922 and 1923, against any Olympic squad of that era, with the exception of the Americans, who routinely vanquished their European opponents by equally massive goal spreads. In 1924, the Granites demolished Czechoslovakia 30–0, and Watson scored a hat trick in the first period, six goals in the second and two more in the third; and the games were only three periods of 15 minutes each. Still, this wasn't his most rewarding match. In a 33–0 steamroll over Switzerland, Watson scored 13 times, an Olympic ice hockey record. Their toughest match came against USA for the gold. Canada recorded a convincing 6–1 win, with Watson scoring three times. As good as he was, Watson never gave up his amateur status, unlike lesser-skilled teammates Hooley Smith and Dunc Munro, both of whom later made their names in the NHL. For Watson, his five remarkable Olympic games in 1924 brought him more than enough glory. Few players have been honoured by both the Hockey Hall of Fame and the IIHF Hall of Fame, but there he is among a handful of double inductees, including Vladislav Tretiak, Borje Salming and Jari Kurri.

6.25   B. 22 players

As hat tricks go, this threesome may just be the most elusive to score. As of 2009, only 22 players have membership in the Triple Gold Club, the ultra-exclusive fraternity for champions of the Olympics, World Championships and Stanley Cup. Given the few opportunities North American NHLers once had for Olympic play, most club members come from Europe, including nine Swedes, six Russians and two Czechs. Only five Canadians qualify, but no Americans. Nor are there any goaltenders, with six defensemen and 16 forwards in the club. The first members were Tomas Jonsson, Mats Naslund and Hakan Loob in 1994, followed by Valeri Kamensky, Alexei Gusarov, Peter Forsberg, Viacheslav Fetisov, Igor Larionov, Alexander Mogilny, Vladimir Malakhov, Rob Blake, Joe Sakic, Brendan Shanahan, Scott Niedermayer, Jaromir Jagr, Jiri Slegr, Nicklas Lidstrom, Fredrik Modin, Chris Pronger, Niklas Kronwall, Henrik Zetterberg and Mikael Samuelsson. Only Forsberg, Fetisov and Larionov have won each of the three championships more than once; and the Detroit Red Wings have contributed an NHL-high eight members to the Triple Gold Club.

6.26 D. 46 goals scored; two goals allowed
Women's hockey among competing Olympic nations today is eerily reminiscent of early men's hockey during the 1920s and 1930s. Back then, high-scoring games were standard, and most of the goals came at the expense of Canada's much weaker opponents. Similarly, there was some inevitability about the outcome in women's hockey at the 2006 Olympics. Canada, as defending champion, cruised to glory and another gold by dominating the opposition in all five games, including the final match against the tournament's biggest surprise, Sweden. Canada's women methodically demolished Italy 16–0, Russia 12–0 and Sweden 8–1 in the round robin; then set their sites on Finland with a 6–0 semi-final win and a 4–1 victory against the Swedes to clinch the gold medal. The tally? Canada outscored its opposition 46–2 and outplayed them by a margin of 193 to 59 shots on goal. But the Canadians never once faced their arch-enemy, USA, as Sweden upset the Americans in a bold shootout victory that saw 19-year-old goaltender Kim Martin stop 37 of 39 shots and all four shootout attempts in the 3–2 semi-final win. It was considered the biggest upset in women's hockey and set the stage for the first ever championship final not involving a USA-Canada showdown.

6.27 D. More than US$12,000
While the whereabouts of Paul Henderson's 1972 Summit Series-winning puck was only recently settled, no mystery

ever surrounded the rubber disc that Mike Eruzione potted in USA's 4–3 shocker against the Soviets at the 1980 Olympics. The puck that changed hockey history was finally sold in 2003 to Mark Friedland, an Aspen, Colorado businessman who specializes in high-end American memorabilia. Its original owner was Sherburne, New York–native Delmar D. Law Jr., who caught the puck shortly after Eruzione slapped in the famous game-winner. Among the other items in Friedland's possession is Law's game tickets (Section 2, Row K, Seat 1, original price: $56), his official Olympic hat and game program, personal photos of the match and a video showing the puck going from the Soviet net to centre ice for the faceoff, where it was flipped from the ice and into the stands. Friedland bought the puck for a reported US$13,200 and was looking for a bid to sell at US$95,000 in 2004.

6.28 C. Scott Niedermayer

If Scott Niedermayer had started his career any earlier he might have won the Canada Cup as well, but, as it is, he barely has enough shelf space in his rec room for his four commemorative Stanley Cups and all that hardware from his international competitions. He is literally hockey's biggest winner, a title-holder of all six of hockey's most prestigious championships. Besides his Stanley Cups in 1995, 2000 and 2003 with New Jersey and 2007 with Anaheim, Niedermayer has represented Canada and won Olympic gold in 2002, a World Championship and World Cup in 2004 and the World Junior Championship in 1991. In 1991–92 he then made his NHL appearance in four of the Devils' first 22 games and was assigned to the Western Hockey League Kamloops Blazers, with whom he won the Memorial Cup in 1992. And as a measure of his stature internationally: Niedermayer's absence (due to injury) from the 2006 Olympics was cited as one of the main factors behind Canada's poor results at the tournament.

Olympic Mettle

FEW WOULD ARGUE THAT the most anticipated and prestigious Winter Olympic events happen at the rink. Figure skating has a certain lustre but hockey is the jewel of the Games. Since 1998, when NHL players arrived in full force, the Olympics have taken on a new dimension with professionals mixing among amateur athletes. The NHLers below have won Olympic medals dating back to 1984. Match the players and their medal rankings and year. Be careful, some players such as Paul Kariya, have won medals at more than one Olympics. Each player can only be used once.

Solutions are on page 140

1. _____ Gold 2006 – Sweden	A.	Brett Hull
2. _____ Silver 2006 – Finland	B.	Nikolai Khabibulin
3. _____ Bronze 2006 – Czech Rep.	C.	Teemu Selanne
4. _____ Gold 2002 – Canada	D.	Igor Larionov
5. _____ Silver 2002 – USA	E.	Peter Forsberg
6. _____ Bronze 2002 – Russia	F.	Thomas Kaberle
7. _____ Gold 1998 – Czech Rep.	G.	Alexander Mogilny
8. _____ Silver 1998 – Russia	H.	Dominik Hasek
9. _____ Gold 1994 – Sweden	I.	Eric Lindros
10. _____ Silver 1994 – Canada	J.	Teppo Numminen
11. _____ Gold 1992 – Unified Team	K.	Mario Lemieux
12. _____ Silver 1992 – Canada	L.	Pavel Bure
13. _____ Gold 1988 – USSR	M.	Mats Sundin
14. _____ Silver 1988 – Finland	N.	Alexei Yashin
15. _____ Gold 1984 – USSR	O.	Paul Kariya

SOLUTIONS TO GAMES

GAME 1 The Triple Gold Club

	OLYMPICS	WORLD CHAMPIONSHIPS	STANLEY CUP
Nicklas Lidstrom	2006	1991	1997
Brendan Shanahan	2002	1994	1997
Jaromir Jagr	1998	2005	1991
Alexander Mogilny	1988	1989	2000
Joe Sakic	2002	1994	1996
Henrik Zetterberg	2006	2006	2008
Hakan Loob	1994	1987	1989
Chris Pronger	2002	1997	2007
Peter Forsberg	1994	1992	1996
Igor Larionov	1984	1982	1997

GAME 2 Summit Series Sayings

1. Anatoli Tarasov
2. Serge Savard
3. Alexander Gusev
4. Phil Esposito
5. Pete Mahovlich
6. Yuri Liapkin
7. Viktor Kuzkin
8. Valeri Kharlamov
9. Alan Eagleson

GAME 3 Twist of Fate

1. In 1935, Czech coaches were so impressed with MIKE BUCKNA, they invited him to coach their national team and organize their hockey system. He coached the Czech team to the 1947 World Championship and a silver medal at the 1948 Olympics. He is credited with not only developing the Czech playbook but advancing the game across Europe.

2. When Team Canada arrived home victorious from Moscow after 1972's Summit Series, SERGE SAVARD played a practical joke on his good friend and assistant coach John Ferguson, by giving away his hockey stick autographed by every player on Team Canada. Ferguson had guarded the stick all the way home from Moscow, but could say nothing when Savard offered it as a gift to Prime Minister Pierre Trudeau.

3. Incredible but true, KARIL YUGOROV, the Soviet PA announcer in Moscow at 1972's Summit Series between Canada and the Soviet Union, was actually Carl Watts, a Canadian citizen, born on a small farm in southern Manitoba. Several years prior to 1972, Yugorov had immigrated to the Soviet Union, where his parents were originally from. He and his brother George both became well-known broadcasters in Russia.

4. Swedish goalie KIM MARTIN was only 15 years old when she made 32 saves in a 2–1 upset over Finland for bronze at the 2002 Olympics. It was Sweden's first-ever medal in top-level competition in women's hockey.

5. Twins FRANTISEK AND ZDENEK TIKAL were separated in 1948 after Zdenek defected from their native Czechoslovakia. The hockey-playing siblings never saw each other again until they met in a 1960 Olympic game— Frantisek playing for the Czech national team and Zdenek suiting up for a squad from Australia. Interestingly, a collision between the two during game action sidelined Zdenek with a separated shoulder. The brothers never got the chance to speak to each other with the Czech secret police watching over Frantisek's every move during the event.

6. VASILY TIKHONOV became the first Russian coach in the history of North American pro hockey when he assumed command of the IHL's Kansas City Blades in October 1995. Tikhonov's father was legendary Soviet coach Viktor Tikhonov.

7. Salt Lake City's STEVE KONOWALCHUK of the Washington Capitals was one of 37 players invited to the U.S. camp but the nine-year NHL veteran was forced to miss the 2002 Olympics in his hometown after being sidelined with reconstructive surgery on his shoulder in October 2001.

8. Dutchman BRAM VAN DER STOK, a member of the Netherlands team that went to the 1935 World Championship, was captured during World War II and became a prisoner of war at Stalag Luft III camp, where he took part in the infamous "Great Escape." Of the 75 escapees, only three prisoners avoided recapture, including van der Stok.

GAME 4 The Granites, Mercurys and Smoke Eaters

1. 1924 – Toronto
2. 1934 – Saskatoon
3. 1935 – Winnipeg
4. 1936 – Port Arthur
5. 1937 – Kimberley
6. 1938 – Sudbury
7. 1948 – RCAF
8. 1950 – Edmonton
9. 1954 – Whitby
10. 1956 – Kitchener-Waterloo

F. Granites
C. Quakers
J. Monarchs
H. Bearcats
B. Dynamiters
I. Wolves
E. Flyers
A. Mercurys
D. Dunlops
G. Dutchmen

GAME 5 Storming the NHL

1. Alexander Ovechkin leads all Europeans with 528 shots in 2008–09.
2. Peter and Anton Stastny scored eight points each on February 22, 1981 to lead all Europeans for most points in one game.
3. Dominik Hasek set an NHL-record 13 shutouts by a European goalie in 1997–98.
4. Alexander Mogilny and Teemu Selanne each scored 76 goals in 1992–93, the highest total ever by European players.

5. Teemu Selanne scored 76 goals in 1992–93, the most goals by a rookie in one season.
6. Paul Stastny holds the rookie record for longest consecutive point-scoring streak with 20 straight games in 2006–07.
7. Evgeni Nabokov and Arturs Irbe lead all European goalies with 77 games each; Nabokov in 2007–08 and Irbe in 2000–01.
8. Peter Forsberg and Jari Kurri lead all Europeans with five points in one period.
9. Sergei Fedorov recorded an NHL-high 29 overtime points, as of 2008–09.
10. Jaromir Jagr scored 646 career goals, the most by a European right winger.
11. Nicklas Lidstrom leads all European scorers with 18 overtime assists, as of 2008–09.
12. Jari Kurri scored a record-tying 19 goals in the 1985 playoffs.

GAME 6 Olympic Mettle

1. Gold 2006 · Sweden
2. Silver 2006 · Finland
3. Bronze 2006 · Czech Rep.
4. Gold 2002 · Canada
5. Silver 2002 · USA
6. Bronze 2002 · Russia
7. Gold 1998 · Czech Rep.
8. Silver 1998 · Russia
9. Gold 1994 · Sweden
10. Silver 1994 · Canada
11. Gold 1992 · Unified Team
12. Silver 1992 · Canada
13. Gold 1988 · USSR
14. Silver 1988 · Finland
15. Gold 1984 · USSR

M. Mats Sundin
C. Teemu Selanne
F. Thomas Kaberle
K. Mario Lemieux
A. Brett Hull
N Alexei Yashin
H. Dominik Hasek
L. Pavel Bure
E. Peter Forsberg
O. Paul Kariya
B. Nikolai Khabibulin
I. Eric Lindros
G. Alexander Mogilny
J. Teppo Numminen
D. Igor Larionov

ACKNOWLEDGEMENTS

Thanks to the following publishers and organizations for the use of quoted and/or statistical material:

· IIHF *Top 100 Hockey Stories of All-Time* (2008) by Szymon Szemberg and Andrew Podnieks. Published by Fenn Publishing Company Ltd.
· *Canada on Ice* (2008) by Dave Holland. Published by Canada On Ice Productions.
· *The World Cup of Hockey* (2003) by Joe Pelletier. Published by Warwick Publishing Inc.

- *Cold War* (1996) by Roy MacSkimming. Published by Greystone Books.
- *World of Hockey* (2007) edited by Szymon Szemberg and Andrew Podnieks. Published by Fenn Publishing Company Ltd.
- *The Days Canada Stood Still* (1992) by Scott Morrison. Published by Warwick Publishing Group.
- *When the Lights Went Out* (2006) by Gare Joyce. Published by Doubleday Canada.
- *Long Shot* (2007) by Eric Zweig. Published by James Lorimer & Company Ltd.
- *Total Hockey* (1998, 2000) and *Total NHL* (2003) by Dan Diamond and Associates Inc. Published by Total Sports.
- *Kings of the Ice* (2002) by Andrew Podnieks and others. Published by NDE Publishing.
- *The Hockey News*, various excerpts. A division of Transcontinental Media G.P.
- *The National Hockey League Official Guide and Record Book* (various years), by the National Hockey League. Published by Dan Diamond and Associates Inc.

Also, the *Globe and Mail, Montreal Gazette, National Post, London Free Press, Toronto Star, Canadian Press, Sports Illustrated* and numerous other publications; databases such as Hockey Summary Project and The Internet Hockey Database; documentaries such as *Summit on Ice;* television networks; and Internet sources, such as nhl.com, iihf.com, 1972summitseries.com, hsp.flyershistory.net, hhof.com, thehockeynut. com, russianhockey.net, azhockey.com, chidlovski.com and trailsmokeeaters.ca that both guided and corroborated our research.

Care has been taken to trace ownership of copyright material contained in this book. The publishers welcome any information that will enable them to rectify any reference or credit in subsequent editions.

The author gratefully acknowledges all the help from everyone at *The Hockey News;* Phil Prichard and Craig Campbell at the Hockey Hall of Fame; Gary Meagher and Benny Ercolani of the NHL; Joanie Agler at the International Tennis Hall of Fame & Museum; the staff at the McLellan-Redpath Library at McGill University; friend and colleague Rob Sanders and Susan Rana at Greystone Books; the many hockey writers, broadcast journalists, media and Internet organizations who have made the game better through their own work; as well as editor Derek Fairbridge, proofreader Hazel Boydell and designers Peter Cocking and Heather Pringle, for their dedication, expertise and creativity. Special thanks to Joe Pelletier for making all those saucer passes to help keep my facts correct.

PHOTO CREDITS